# NO MORE 24/7

## ENTREPRENEURS, TAKE YOUR LIFE BACK

### CATHERINE COWART ROE

Cypress Bayou Press, LLC

ISBN 979-8-9923678-0-5 (print)
ISBN 979-8-9923678-1-2 (ebook)

catherine@cowartroe.com
catherinecowartroe.com

Production Management: Weaving Influence, Inc.
Cover and Interior Design: Rachel Royer
Developmental Editing: Anjanette Harper
Copyediting: Meredith Mix
Typesetting: Lori Weidert
Proofreading: Keri Hales

Printed in the United States of America

*For Miriam*

# Contents

# Chapter 3

## STRUCTURED SCHEDULING ..........................................27

# Chapter 4

## COMMUNICATION BOUNDARIES ...........................45

# Chapter 5

## MANAGEMENT TOOLS
## AND AUTOMATION

# Chapter 6

## MULTITASKING

# Chapter 7

## BE FLEXIBLE

# Chapter 8

## WHEN TO HIRE

# Chapter 9

## WORKLOAD ALLOCATION

# Chapter 10

## EVALUATION

# Chapter 11

## DON'T PROCRASTINATE

# Chapter 12

## FATAL COMBO

# Chapter 1
## Stop Being On Call

"You're glued to that thing."

I stared down at my phone and paused to look up. Once again, I had been sucked into my email inbox. I was sending a "quick" response to a client. It was only a few seconds.

"Did you even hear what I just said?"

No. I did not hear, and I still could not tell you today what my dad said. My daughter, who spent school afternoons with him, pulled on my arm to get my attention away from that thing I was staring at. It had been several minutes I had been on my phone, not seconds.

When I had my daughter, I quit my full-time corporate accountant position and took my solo CPA firm full-time so I could spend more time with her. But what quality was that time? When I picked her up at my dad's after school, he'd stand right next to me and try to ask me a question; I would ignore him because I *had* to finish writing an email.

Dad was right. I never put my phone down. If I had lost it, my life would have been over. I always dreaded opening the screen time app on my phone. It would send weekly alerts, hard statistical data of my overconsumption. If asked to describe how I felt, it was guilt. I had to check off those tasks. I had to set up that account. I had to answer that email. People were waiting.

I would justify being on the phone at lunch with my family or periodically checking in at times when I was off work, not even because I got an alert or notification. I was just checking to see if there was one. I felt guilty about the freedom I found with my flexible work hours. I told myself things like, "If I had a more traditional work schedule then I would be working now anyway," or "I need to at least seem like I am working right now." I wasn't working 40 hours a week. It was closer to 50, more if you include the time I spent jumping on and off the phone.

I slowly began to realize that this was not the lifestyle I intended when I started a business. I created this business so I could have more flexibility with work, not less. I could not keep living this way. I knew that I needed to make some big changes, but it would be worth it.

## BUSINESS IS GREAT! BUT I FEEL SO BAD

Do you feel guilty when you unplug from technology? Do you feel like you need to check in on your business during your off time, even when you are with family? Perhaps your family members have complained that you aren't mentally present. Have you tried to multitask your way to achievement only to create a mess of unfinished or poorly completed tasks and unaccomplished goals?

Do you feel like you work all the time, whether you work eight hours a day or 5? You didn't start a business so you could work all the time. Maybe you became an entrepreneur because you had a service to provide and a passion for solving problems, but now you are overserving—at your own expense. Or you started a business so you could work your way on your terms, but now the business is running you. You wanted freedom, but you are enslaved to what once was your passion.

You want to be a successful business owner, but you realize that something needs to change.

This is not your fault!

Technological advances have created instant access to anyone and anything. The pressure to always be on call combined with that instant access pushes entrepreneurs to work all the time. Society dictates that entrepreneurs need to be available 24/7 to run their businesses successfully. This is not true! Working all the time will not make you more efficient. Being on call for your business is undermining your success. The solution is to set and maintain boundaries for work. This is how you can take back your life and reclaim your freedom while becoming more efficient and successful than before.

## WHERE DID THE 40-HOUR WORK WEEK COME FROM?

You're probably wondering why you should care about the work week. Let me ask a question. Can you honestly say that you only work nine to five, Monday through Friday? No? Why not? Isn't that the standard? Somehow, society got off track. Understanding the history of how work schedules evolved may help us discover where the work train derailed.

The traditional 5-day, 40-hour work week was first implemented by Henry Ford of Ford Motor Company in 1926, only a few years before the stock market crash that resulted in the Great Depression. In 1938, President Franklin D. Roosevelt signed the Labor Standards Act into law. This act encompasses various labor-related provisions, including the right to a minimum wage, requiring overtime pay for those exceeding 40 hours of work per week, and regulations concerning child labor.[1] Prior to this, there were no limitations on working hours. People were overworked, burned out, and riddled with health concerns. Sound familiar?

With these laws in place now, how have we returned to this state of never-ending work? Well, many people are exempt from the Labor Standards Act, including executive, administrative, and professional employees as defined by the Labor Standards Act.[2] For consultants, this excludes you and most of your team from protection. Unless you set boundaries for work, you and your employees can easily fall into the trap of constant work.

You may ask, "What is work-life balance?" People use this term so often, and everyone seems to have a different definition for it. Well, the term "work-life balance" was first used in the U.S. in the 1980s, at the peak of the Women's Liberation Movement. During this time, maternity leave and flexible work schedules were created to support women in the workplace.[3] The concept was intended to protect women in the workforce and promote equality. This was designed to allow for flexibility with work to align with your personal life, not the other way around! Now, people feel obligated to take work home. If you work from home, work is home, and home is work. There are no lines to blur. There's just chaos.

According to research from the U.S. Bureau of Labor 2021 Business Response Survey, 50 percent of work between April and December of 2020 was performed remotely. Prior to the COVID-19 pandemic, 5 percent was remote.[4] This is a big deal! Remote work and the concept of working from home were taboo or rarely used, outside-the-norm practices prior to the COVID-19 pandemic. Because of the pandemic shutdowns in 2020, many businesses were forced to reevaluate their practices and adapt to remote work. When businesses were told to shut down in-person operations, they threw together remote-work plans and sent their employees off into isolation with the same deadlines and the same target goals as before. We went from hardly ever working remotely to remote work becoming a staple in society overnight.

Technology has made this possible. Over the past twenty years, workforce communication has expanded to include work text messages and email apps on your phone. Now, people send emails asking for a meeting that same day. Now, people call five times a day if you don't answer. Now, you get countless spam calls and emails every day. These technological advances in communication drive us to work all the time. The COVID-19 pandemic added fuel. Now, you are expected to check your email at your kid's soccer game or log in virtually to finish a report after dinner.

According to a *Forbes* survey, as of 2023, 12.7 percent of full-time workers work from home, and 28.8 percent have a hybrid work setup combining both in-office and work-from-home arrangements.[5] This shows that, even though the pandemic has calmed down, virtual work is still very popular. Remote work doesn't seem to be going anywhere.

Today, people can now work anywhere, anytime. The COVID-19 pandemic of 2020, along with increasing technological abilities and the normalization of remote work, have destroyed the separation of work and life. This constant availability quickly transforms "anywhere, anytime" into "everywhere, all the time." Society demands that you are always on, ready at a moment's notice.

Again, this is not your fault! Society is telling you that you need to be available at any given time. It can be incredibly difficult to push back. This is the new reality, but this does not have to be true for you! Believe it or not, being on call for your business is undermining your success. Setting and maintaining boundaries for work are key for taking back your life.

In this book I will show you that you don't have to go along with the status quo. It takes time and practice, but you can stand up for your free time. This shift will take some time to get used to, as well as take some trial and error to find what works best for you. I understand that this is a lot to take in. Don't worry! I will be your guide on this journey.

## WHAT DO SUCCESSFUL ENTREPRENEURS DO?

Successful entrepreneurs don't work 24/7, nor are they available at any given time.

- They set and maintain clear boundaries.
- They prioritize their work based on how their minds work.
- They hire, allocate, and outsource when possible.
- They set goals and plans to be consistent.

- They avoid overestimating their capacity and underestimating their value.
- They take breaks and vacations and do self-care activities.
- They practice when to say yes and when to say no.
- They limit their availability so they can be fully present.
- They know that they need to be healthy physically, mentally, and spiritually.

And most important of all, they make self-care a high priority, knowing that they need to replenish the source—themselves. They take societal expectations with a grain of salt and reject agendas pushed onto them as "fact." They use their own knowledge and experience to decide what is best for their businesses, their families, and themselves.

## DATE NIGHT DISASTER

One Saturday evening around 5:00 p.m., Kevin, a fellow CPA firm owner, was walking into a restaurant for date night with his wife, Tracey, after what had been a long, hard week for both of them. He received two missed calls from a client, the wife of a husband-wife business duo. He was worried that she would call repetitively if he didn't respond, so texted her saying he was on a date with his wife. He even asked her to let him know what she needed so he could take care of it on Monday. The client responded with a long message, completely disregarding the fact that he was out on a Saturday evening. Her husband's driver's license had been suspended due to an outstanding tax liability, but they were leaving town the next day. Now they didn't know if he would be able to fly.

Kevin sat at a dinner table across from his wife on his phone, actively engaging with these people via text message. He told the client that there was nothing he could do about this on a Saturday night anyway but that he could investigate it on Monday. The client ignored this and responded again with a long text message that implied it was Kevin's fault!

Over the course of three hours, Kevin stayed engaged with the clients, finding and sending screenshots that showed this wasn't his fault or responsibility, all while sitting at dinner with his wife. Tracey was furious that this other woman was more of a priority on a Saturday night than she, Kevin's wife. She wished that Kevin had never texted the client back. No amount of money was worth that treatment, and they couldn't get their date night back.

A few months passed by, and Kevin was one working day before the tax deadline. The same client started texting at 9:30 in the morning, back-to-back random ideas in a last-minute effort to try to reduce the tax owed with the return. Kevin responded initially, informing them that some of their suggestions did not apply to them and others they did not qualify for at all. Each time, she replied with explanations of why she thought she could get certain deductions. Kevin stopped responding because, as time went on, the messages didn't require a response or changes to answer.

At the end of the workday, Kevin received a message from them saying, "Hey, we're used to being able to get on the phone with our previous CPA or his assistant and ask questions whenever we're making decisions, and you know, we just like to get some more communication from you." She continued to argue that she had questions here and there and was used to getting clarification over the phone at any given time.

Kevin informed them, "I don't offer always-on availability."

The client responded with, "Okay, we didn't realize that was separate. Let's get the quote on that because we don't want to miss anything."

Historically, Kevin's clients would call, text, and send emails periodically. He would be in touch when he was available. Everything seemed fine. He never had any complaints. Kevin realized after these two incidents that this client was not going to be a good fit for him. They wanted him to be available to them all the time. They selfishly disregarded his time away from work to be with his family. They expected him to be at their beck and call even though he has a life and other clients.

Kevin struggled to disengage from that disrespectful client. This client was one of the first he signed when he started his business, so it was difficult for him to let go of a business relationship he had for so long. He combated additional fears surrounding the loss of revenue and uncertainty about ending the engagement. Those fears were exacerbated because he had recently taken his part-time accounting practice full-time. Growing a new business involves a lot of uncertainty, so it can be scary to let clients go, especially large ones that produce regular recurring revenue. Kevin also knew that he would still encounter the client in everyday life, as they ran in the same circles in a very small town. Ending business engagements with people you are still involved with can be very intimidating.

He finally let go of his fear of losing that client and what that would mean for him and his business. Letting go of that fear allowed Kevin to change the way he operates his business. He created a list of internal boundaries that limit his interactions with clients outside working hours and planned how to serve clients without affecting his family life. These steps keep clients from walking over him. He focuses more on vetting his clients and is more particular with the clients he takes. He no longer gives his cell phone number to clients. He has decided that there is no price tag that can be put on having an uninterrupted Saturday evening dinner with his wife.

Kevin now has available space in his business calendar to take on newer, more appreciative, and less demanding clients. He may be losing out on potential revenue from the original client, but he has the availability to find someone better to work with. He has also learned that his family time and sanity are more valuable to him than the loss of revenue, even though his business is in a startup, growth-oriented stage.

## NOT WORKING 24/7 GIVES FREEDOM

Not working around the clock provides you the freedom to live a well-balanced life, stay healthy, keep positive relationships, make better decisions, and overall live life feeling accomplished and fulfilled. By balancing work and life, you will find that you have more time and focus for yourself. You can use more of your time to enjoy hobbies, spend quality time with your family and friends, and take care of your physical and mental health. You will feel complete satisfaction during your time away from work without worrying about work. You will know what time you have committed to your work life and are committed to keeping that separate from your personal life. Living in the mindset of not working all the time significantly reduces burnout. You will make better decisions and find that you are more creative and innovative because you have flexibility and work at a more sustainable pace over the long term.

I am asking you to change your mindset about how you view and react to the work expectations of our modern society. Picture a life where you can go to your kid's swim meet and not worry about the client who emailed you three times in a row that they need a meeting ASAP. Picture a life where you can plan out your day and feel accomplished at the end of it because you didn't jump from task to task but instead got something done. This is freedom.

Today, I no longer sit on my phone all day. Sometimes, I even turn it off and have hours of uninterrupted time to do anything but check in. I work only when I have planned to work and am considerably more productive with the work that I am doing. My work time is work time, and my off time is off time. It sounds simple to say, but it is very difficult to apply. If I get an email while I am eating lunch or walking around the zoo, it can wait. Honestly, I can say that I do still feel the urge to check in. I actively resist opening an email when it comes through, but I know that my life will be more productive if I save that for later.

## WHAT ARE YOUR FEARS?

You are reading this book because you are tired of always being on call. You want a solution. You recognize that following societal expectations is not working for you, but you are afraid to make changes. This is completely normal. Making a change can be a scary thing, especially when the change involves your livelihood and your reputation. Realizing that you need to change is not always a sudden moment of epiphany.

I had very similar fears when I adjusted how I work and live my life. For me, it was a buildup of choices that I realized were sucking my life away. The main factors that affected me were being glued to my phone, the email infinity loop, and my arguments with my mom about distractions. These weren't one-time events either. They were recurring. It took some time for me to really admit that this was a problem and decide to make changes.

I will admit that I was in denial for a while. What's important is I did realize that I needed to change and took steps to make those changes.

Realizing a need for change isn't always instantaneous! Changing your overall mindset toward how you approach work and life does not happen overnight either. This is true for me and is true for you. Many of these challenges and struggles will continue to be just as challenging and frustrating even after you implement your changes. I still struggle with my challenges every day. I still constantly feel pulled to check my e-mail or check my phone as soon as I get a notification. I try my hardest to follow my plan and avoid giving in to those temptations, but I still do it sometimes. I'm not perfect, and neither are you. Every bit of effort counts. Slip-ups here and there make you human, but staying in a mindset that is counterproductive to your success as an entrepreneur is detrimental to your life and your business. I have learned to harness my fear of failure as motivation to press on and overcome these temptations. You can too! Practicing these techniques consistently will quieten those voices telling you to give in and check that notification. This will get easier with time.

Most importantly, remember that this is not your fault. You have so much noise in your head, pulling you in a million different directions. Society is throwing information and instructions at you relentlessly. You are a victim of the system, just like me. By reading this book, you are realizing that as well. This is the biggest, possibly even the most challenging, step forward for you. You are committing to changing your life for the better and freeing yourself, and that effort alone is commendable.

## FEAR: I FEEL GUILTY

We feel guilty about setting and holding boundaries, to the point that we feel like we need to put ourselves second to everyone else. Ayn Rand, a Russian-American writer and philosopher, created a term for this: unearned guilt.[6] This is a feeling of guilt for something that you are not responsible for or have no control over. We feel like if we can only take care of everyone else's needs, then we can finally rest and take care of ourselves. Don't get me wrong here: caring for other people is a great value. Still, you also must understand that you can only do so much. You can do more for other people if you have taken better care of yourself. Recognizing that these feelings stem from unearned guilt will help you face this fear.

## FEAR: I DON'T HAVE THE TIME OR RESOURCES

The fear that you don't have the time is very common. I want to show that you do have time—and more time than you think. Taking the time now to change your mindset and resist nonstop work is the key to having more time in the future to create the freedom you want in your life. If you set boundaries and stick to them, you will have more time than you could imagine. Many of the tools that we are going to review are one-time-only tasks. Setting up new processes does take time but once you get on a roll, your new work processes will become second nature to you.

## FEAR: I DON'T WANT TO BE REJECTED OR CONFRONTED

What if my clients completely reject my boundaries or confront them? This is going to happen. Pushback against boundaries is human nature. People are going to test the limits.  They are going to continue to try things that have worked in the past. The change must come from your actions and reactions in these situations. Eventually your clients will learn that either they abide by your rules, or they will move on elsewhere. More likely than not, they will learn to respect your boundaries. If they don't respect your boundaries, then I'd like you to think hard and consider if you really want them as clients.

## MY PROMISE

You may currently be living in the mindset that being available 24/7 is necessary to be a successful entrepreneur. I am telling you the opposite. In this book, I am asking you to change your mindset. I will show you skills and tactics you can use to take back your life, such as keeping a structured schedule, planning personal care, setting and maintaining boundaries, utilizing time management and productivity tools, hiring and work allocation, evaluating your business, and maintaining consistency. This book provides the framework and layout of exactly what you need to do so you can regain control of how and when you work. I am here as your guide to relieve your fears! Live your life to the fullest. Don't be reduced to the status quo. When you embrace the practice of setting boundaries, you will find freedom. By the end of this book, you will take back your life so you can be more successful and efficient than before.

# Chapter 2
## Understanding Your Bandwidth

Megan never intended to start a coaching business. It just happened. She was very successful, and her business grew exponentially. Generally, Megan loves to work and loves the very nature of her work. But because her business did not grow slowly and steadily, an extra level of stress began to build in her life.

As she put it, "So look at NFL players, right? They're always on the injured list. They know that, at some point when they're in their 50s, they're going to be limping no matter what. They're not going to be active in their 70s because they're beating their bodies up. . . . We were doing the same thing because I was aware of how much I was hurting myself, but I wanted to be there, and nothing was going to stop me. I put on an arm brace or knee brace and took a steroid shot to do whatever I could to stay in the game, knowing good and well that I was already hurting."

She continued, "By being in pain, I wasn't able to perform my best, but I just hid it from everyone. I kept going, potentially risking further damage and further injury. I was going to push myself until I broke, and in that process, see everyone around me break, too, because people were counting on me."

Megan began to develop physical symptoms not just of physical strain but of stress. They started with stomach pains. She would hear the "ding" of a notification on her phone and feel pain. Eventually, she realized that she had been having bad stomach pains for several days. The longevity of this episode caused her to question her overall health. She had a panic attack for two days straight. It did not stop her from working, though, because working was more important.

After those two days of hell, Megan realized that she could not keep living this way. Work was killing her! She took her time and carefully made her decision to pull back. Today, while she still wants to do a lot of work, the clientele she's focusing on brings a significantly lower level of stress and more lax expectations.

Taking a step back and evaluating her mental health has been freeing for Megan. She started out using her mental capacity almost exclusively for work, leaving very little bandwidth for anything else, including her health. Megan realized she shouldn't feel beat up and ready to retire like a middle-aged football player.

Do you also feel like Megan? Maybe you have been "injured" but felt pressured to do whatever it took to "stay in the game." We all need to manage our mental bandwidth to avoid falling out of the game or into premature retirement.

## WHAT IS MENTAL BANDWIDTH?

People, like computers, have a finite amount of processing power in their brains. Mental bandwidth is part of that processing power. It consists of the cognitive resources and capabilities the human brain has to process information and make decisions. This describes the limited nature of our mental capacity and how we allocate that capacity to various tasks and activities.

According to *Everyday Bandwidth*, our brains can process approximately 11 million bits of information per second, and the bandwidth we have for processing is about 100 bits.[7] I don't want you to memorize bits, but I do want you to know that this is a tangible, measurable process, not a metaphorical concept. Our mental capacity is limited, so we need to manage our cognitive functioning to be our best selves! There are many factors that can play a part in our mental bandwidth.

The complexity of individual tasks affects our mental load. More complex and challenging activities require more bandwidth than easier activities. The practice of multitasking and bouncing back and forth between tasks reduces the mental capacity available for each activity, which causes lower performance overall. Stress, anxiety, and other extreme or particularly negative emotions can drain your mental capacity. This makes it more difficult to complete anything, regardless of the complexity. Personal care, such as sleep, rest, and nutrition, affects your mental capacity and functioning. Prioritizing work according to your available bandwidth will help you work more efficiently.

Managing your mental bandwidth helps you become more productive, feel better, and make better decisions. Everyone has different levels of mental capacity and different skill sets, making it impossible to design a formula for how your brain works. Personal evaluation and understanding of your mental capacity are required.

These changes do not have to be major changes to have a major impact on your life. For example, understanding my bandwidth has helped me make better decisions in many areas of my life. By my second semester in college, I learned that I should not take 8:00 a.m. classes. My mind was just not there. Once I stopped scheduling classes that early, my sleep improved, my energy increased, and my memory was stronger. What are some changes you could make to feel better?

## WHAT IS COGNITIVE MANAGEMENT?

I constantly hear various business coaches and business planning experts talk about time management as being the key to success in business. Time management is important, but cognitive management comes first. People talk about time because it is clearly defined and easy to plan. Time is the same for everyone. There are only 24 hours in a day, 7 days in a week. Nobody argues with that. On the other hand, your mental capacity for your workload is specific to you and requires effort on your part to measure it properly. Measuring your bandwidth involves a great amount of effort because each person is so vastly different; this is truly a personalized experience.

Think about each activity that you perform on a regular basis. Some activities require more mental energy from you than others. Doing laundry requires very minimal mental effort and can probably be done before or after a more complex activity like performing a project analysis. Performing many complex activities back-to-back can lead to burnout regardless of how much time you have available to work on each.

Economics professor Sendhil Mullainathan and behavioral scientist Eldar Shafir together reviewed a study where one school was located near noisy train tracks. The students on the side closest to the noise did not perform as well as the students on the other side of the school.[8] Shafir claims that scarcity is a state in which people don't have sufficient resources, including time or money, along with other essential needs, to meet their needs and fulfill goals. In this case, the students experienced scarcity from the noisy train and didn't achieve their goals. See, the concept of scarcity impacts two specific elements of bandwidth. It affects your ability to reason and problem solve as well as make decisions. Greater scarcity decreases productivity. Scarcity is more than the tangible tools necessary, such as money and physical resources. True scarcity involves your time and mental capacity.

Do you sometimes feel as though you are working near the train tracks? Is something pulling you away from your focus? Everything you do is affected by scarcity, including cognitive functioning and overall decision-making. Shafir's research shows that when people experience scarcity, their ability to make good decisions and perform self-control is greatly impaired.[9]

So often, people misinterpret the effects of scarcity as a need to work longer or harder. This is an ineffective approach to increase productivity. It will only tax your bandwidth even more. So if working harder and longer doesn't work, what will? Search for ways to capitalize on your bandwidth and make rest and recovery a part of your process. Think of the bigger picture. This long-term mindset will help you make decisions that will increase your health as opposed to overworking yourself. Sometimes, when you are struggling, what you need is less, not more. Doesn't that sound refreshing? After all, how much of *you* do you have to go around? Know your limits.

## WHAT IS COGNITIVE OVERLOAD?

In 1968, R. C. Atkinson and R. M. Shiflrin conducted a study on human memory and determined that memory consists of two major elements: memory structure and control processes.[10] Memory structure consists of the permanent components of the system, while control processes are flexible and more situational. Memory structure is like the hardware and physical framework of a computer, and the control processes are the programs and applications it uses. Your brain is basically a computer. Remember, your mind can only process so many bits of info at a time, just like a computer.

Memory can further be broken down into three elements: the sensory register that brings in information, the short-term memory store, and the long-term memory store.

1. The sensory register filters out information and passes on relevant information to your short-term memory to be processed further. Anything not used is typically forgotten.

2. The short-term memory either eliminates the information or stores it in your long-term memory.

3. Long-term memory holds information in categories called schemas that arrange the information according to how we use it.

The more often we use our stored information, the more organized it becomes, and retrieval becomes easier.

Cognitive load is the amount of information that our working memory can process effectively at any time. This theory explains how it is easier to pick up and get back into tasks that we routinely work on as opposed to tasks that we do periodically. It's always generally easier and faster to start and complete tasks that we do daily, weekly, and even monthly. Tasks that are done on a quarterly or annual basis take significantly longer because we must hone in on our long-term memory, remember how to do what we need to do, and then make it happen.

## WHY IS COGNITIVE MANAGEMENT IMPORTANT?

Your brain can only handle so much. The amount that your brain can handle, though, is different from the next person. Because of this, to fully understand how your brain works and processes information, we use cognitive management. This is very similar to time management, as we use a lot of the same tools for both. It's important to know how your brain operates and processes because this determines how much you can do; what types of activities and tasks you should do; at what times of the day; and under what circumstances. There is no perfect or exact formula. You may know that one task is easier done in the morning, but if something comes up in the morning, you will have to readjust everything. It is a great idea to analyze how your brain responds to different tasks so you can try to adjust your schedule based on that information.

The best part of cognitive management is that you aren't tied to time. Here, you analyze based on your ability, and then you can factor time in later. This helps you find ways to become more efficient without increasing time and effort. Instead of increasing the time that you spend on a task or trying to force yourself to work harder in a shorter amount of time, you find the best scenario for your tasks to be as efficient as possible.

# HEADACHE HELL

How do I know if I am mentally overloaded? This is an important question because sometimes it's easier to tell than other times. Some of the signs are physical, but some are mental. The physical ailments are usually easy to see.

One time, I woke up early in the day, and I could tell that I was feeling a little off, but I had a lot of important things that needed to be done. As the day went on, the headache got worse, but I kept pushing harder to try to push through it. By early afternoon, I was driving to pick up my daughter from school, and I had to call my dad and ask him if he could pick her up because I was just so sick. I went right to bed at that point and just lay there for hours, unable to think, unable to move, unable to do anything. Luckily, my dad and daughter had a great afternoon together, but I felt so foolish for ignoring the pain for so long.

Another way mental fatigue can manifest physically is when you feel like you cannot do anything. Going for a jog is the last thing that you think you could do. You aren't physically tired because you were sitting at a computer all day. But while you were sitting at that computer, you were working on some hefty assignments, and you used up your mental energy. Now, you don't have the energy that you otherwise would have for physical activity.

Overload can affect your mental capabilities, as well, especially when you are trying to push through and keep struggling. Mental fatigue can manifest in different ways. A few symptoms of mental overload are brain fog, memory loss, stress, anxiety, inability to focus, and overall mental fatigue. This brain fog that I'm talking about is just generally a haziness where you just feel like you're in a daze, and you can't tell what's going on. Maybe you're struggling to stay in the moment; this leads to an inability to focus and stay on task.

Mental fatigue is different for all of us. When I am just done to my max, unable to do anymore, I get headaches. When I keep pushing to see how much I can get done, they get stronger. If I don't stop and take a step back and notice my symptoms, then I will be incapacitated for a period of time. Understanding the early signs of your mental fatigue is key to knowing when to step back and take care of yourself.

## BRAIN FOG

During tax season, there is a significant amount of time devoted to technical work during the first four months of the year. As we get closer to the deadline, the hours just increase and increase to the point when, on Tax Day, my brain is mush. Today, I can hardly remember anything that happened on Tax Days in past years because I was so overwhelmed and so mentally exhausted. My mind just could not properly function and store any memory from those days.

I remember one tax season when, on Tax Day, I still had five clients who had not signed their returns. After months of emails asking them for information, automated emails about updates, and other forms of communication trying to pull information from these people and get them to review and sign their tax returns, I was completely exhausted. I cared more about filing their taxes than they did.

I was so stressed out and overwhelmed because there was no way that I could let a client go past the deadline. I called people multiple times to remind them. All the emails that I had previously sent were very detailed and included all the deadlines in every single email. I had clients who were still not pressing a button to e-sign their tax return on Tax Day even though they had received at least three emails on different days explaining when the deadline was.

I was still actively engaged, waiting for people all the way up until the middle of the night e-filing deadline. People asked me questions during the day. Some were looking at their tax returns for the first time. They had plenty of time before to do this, but for some reason, it just had not been a priority for them. Their lack of planning became my "emergency." I don't think that these people realized, or even realize to this day, that I was sitting in bed ignoring my family, just staring at the computer past 10:00 p.m. and onward, just waiting to hit a button.

By that point, after working on so many returns under such a stringent timeline, I was a zombie. There was a brain fog of not being completely there, being overworked, and just done. People were pushing last-minute questions on their returns. They didn't realize they were talking to a severely overworked accountant who had not had enough sleep and probably not enough to eat and had been constantly working for the past few weeks. I should not have been working that day! I know that now. By pushing and trying to take care of all these folks, I was putting myself at risk of making mistakes that could be costly. My mental capacity was gone. My cognitive functioning was low because I wasn't managing my abilities.

Now that I have seen the effect of pushing too hard on my body and my mind, I have made some changes. I use my bandwidth better to make sure that I am healthy and my work is done correctly and not completed by an overworked, exhausted person. I have set a rule that all tax returns need to be in their complete stage, whether they are still pending signatures or not, two days before a deadline. This means that I will not be preparing or reviewing tax returns within 48 hours of a tax deadline. Everything has to be done before that. I might be waiting on a signature, and that's okay, because no actual complex, highly involved cognitive thinking should be done during that very stressful, exhausting time, right before the deadline.

I also have created a practice of setting internal deadlines for clients. I have a deadline for when we need to get all the information to ensure timely filing and a deadline for having everything completed. Neither of those deadlines is on Tax Day. This practice has helped manage client expectations of just how far we are willing to push for them, especially if it seems like, sometimes, I care more about completing a client's tax return than they do. This year, I had the least stressful tax season ever in all my years of preparing taxes, and I owe it all to this new way of thinking.

## ONE OF MY DAYS

Right now, in my queue for technical work, I have one tax return that needs to be reviewed and financial statements to review for eight clients. The tax return should be good to go unless I find something that needs to be addressed in my review. However, the financial statements for all the other clients are still pending other information, so they aren't as high of a priority. Knowing this, I am going to work on that tax return first and then each of the other financial statement review tasks in the order that they were sent to me, unless some of the pending information becomes available for any of them. At that point, whichever client has the most complete file will be done first. I also see that I have four 20-minute new-client consults and a 20-minute tax return review session scheduled with a client. All my phone consults are scheduled at the end of the day intentionally because I know from experience that I am mentally fatigued by that part of the day and can handle new client consults, not complex work. I plan to work in the morning, starting with the project that can be completed, reviewing the prepared tax return, and then continuing the projects that aren't quite ready and the financial statement reviews, for as long as time allows. I know that I am not going to perform my best with higher-level tasks in the afternoon and evening and that those are better to be done earlier in the day.

In the afternoon, after using a lot of bandwidth for analytical work, I will do my new-client consults. I know from my experience that I'm not going to do work that requires a higher level of thinking after a day where I have had several back-to-back new-client consults. Sometimes, many lower-level tasks add up and pull from your bandwidth in the same manner that a higher-level task does. This explains why I am so mentally fatigued after a day where I have a lot of client phone calls, especially back-to-back, versus a day where I have one or two sporadically. This shows that there are so many different aspects to look at when considering how everything altogether affects your cognitive functioning.

So far, I have described an actual day with respect to work, not including everyth ing else. It is important for you to remember that your bandwidth is all-encompassing. This is a very big difference between analyzing what you can do based on your mental capacity rather than based on time. You could say that you work eight hours a day, and this is what fits in that time. When you look at your day and your workload capacity for that day solely based on time, you don't factor in what you do outside of that time frame. Analyzing your bandwidth in tandem with time will help you become more efficient and determine when you should do each task.

Aside from work, there are several other factors that affect this day of work that I described. In the morning, I have a 30- to 45-minute run and a one-hour doctor appointment. In the evening, I have a 45-minute dance lesson for my daughter and a short walk with the dog. My morning run is usually a time when I can relax, feel free, and reflect. Many times, I will either create a new idea while running or even solve a problem that I have been pondering for a while. I will most likely use the time during the dance lesson and the dog walk to reflect on the day, plan for the next day, and complete some administrative tasks like tracking time, paying bills, and assigning work to staff. This is very efficient since administrative planning is a simple task for me that can be done with less bandwidth. Also, if I plan the next day ahead of time, I can jump right into my first task at the beginning of the day without wasting time trying to figure out what I am supposed to be working on.

This process helps me use my bandwidth in the most efficient way.

## AIM FOR A STATE OF FLOW

We all want to be happy in everything we do. As an entrepreneur, you have a passion for your business. This is why you started it. Are you truly happy though? If not, are you still searching for the answer? Are you frustrated and ready to give up? When you have so much noise and information thrown at you, finding happiness is a quest that can be easily thrown to the wayside. Who has time for happiness when we're all struggling to get by? These are all terrible thoughts, but we've all had at least some of them. What is the point of creating something or living life if you're just going to work it all away? There has to be some middle ground.

In his search to find the origin of happiness, Mihaly Csikszentmihalyi, a Hungarian-American psychologist, created a concept called flow.[11] Flow is a mental state in which a person is completely engrossed in an activity. This requires great concentration, focused goals, a level of skill and challenge, and a general sense of selflessness. People often forget how much time passes by when they are in this state. When was the last time you felt engrossed in an activity, completely at peace? Csikszentmihalyi discovered that experiencing this phenomenon of flow can increase happiness and overall satisfaction in life because people find a sense of meaning and fulfillment in what they are doing. Flow can exist in activities and tasks that are both work-related and otherwise personal. You can achieve complete satisfaction in your work just like you feel satisfied and doing things you enjoy for leisure. If your business is your passion, think back to what propelled you to start it in the first place.

Csikszentmihalyi's research indicated that the flow state is affected by how much a particular activity challenges you as well as what your skill level is for that activity. Flow exists where the level of challenge the task gives you loosely meets your skill level in performing the activity. Personal growth occurs where your challenge level is high, and your skill level is also high. Fun and ease happen in tasks that are low skill and low in challenge. If a task doesn't challenge you very much, yet you are highly skilled in it, you will become bored. Likewise, if a task is very challenging yet you don't have high skills, you will feel stress and anxiety. The key to experiencing flow is to reach for that fine balance between challenge level and skill level.

## HOW DO I ANALYZE MY COGNITIVE ABILITIES?

The first step is to make a list of all the tasks and activities that you do. This can take some time, so this isn't something that will be done overnight. My suggestion is to start with tasks and activities that you do more frequently, such as on a daily or weekly basis, and then add the more sporadic tasks and activities as you come across them. Once you have a list of activities, identify each as either simple or complex. If you want, you can use additional classifications in between.

Simple activities are activities that come easily to you or don't require too much processing power. Complex activities are activities that require more processing power or are more challenging to you. Vacuuming the house or checking emails are generally simple tasks. Analyzing data or reviewing information with a client are more complex tasks. After labeling tasks as simple or complex, identify if certain activities are generally performed better at certain times of the day. For example, if working out is something that you can only do in the morning, then tag it as a morning task. This is the start to making sure that you don't overpromise what you can do and swear that you can go to the gym in the afternoon when you already know that it's much easier for you to do it in the morning.

At this point, you should be able to understand each task or activity that you do, whether the task is simple or complex, and when is the best time to schedule these tasks. Using both the complexity factor and time of day of all your tasks will give you the best overall big picture of what your daily schedule should consist of.

# Action

Take a few minutes to write out some tasks/activities that you work on during the day, label them as either simple or complex, and then assign a time of day that best fits the activity. We will build on this information later.

Here is an example of my list.

- Run or other workout: SIMPLE—Anytime

- Review tax returns: COMPLEX—Morning

- Review financial statements: COMPLEX—Morning

- Writing a report: COMPLEX—Morning

- New-client consult phone calls: Simple individually, Complex together—Afternoon

- Checking emails: SIMPLE—Evening (if once per day)

- Washing the dishes: SIMPLE—Evening

- Educational webinar: SIMPLE—Anytime

- Administrative tasks: SIMPLE—Anytime

Remember that simple and complex are terms to evaluate your working capacity, not terms to evaluate importance. Importance is a factor of time, not bandwidth. Before deciding how much time to assign to your activities and when to schedule that time, you need to understand how each of these activities affects your bandwidth. Analyzing each activity and your most efficient way to perform it will help you plan the next time.

# Chapter 3
## Structured Scheduling

"Where did all the time go? I feel like I got nothing done today," I hopelessly questioned after a long day of work.

I had gone to the library for the four hours my daughter was at school. I often worked at the library because I enjoyed the peaceful atmosphere, and it was the perfect place to work without interruptions. I could easily work four hours straight on priority, revenue-generating work on any given day.

On this day, I opened my computer, noticed that my email tab was on the screen, and immediately clicked on it. I counted the number of outstanding emails that begged me to review them. I had an unspoken goal to review tax returns during that time block, but I still felt the urge to address these outstanding items. After all, it would only be a few minutes, right?

Once I finished addressing the unread emails, I looked at the clock and realized this cost me 90 minutes of my four-hour priority work time. By the time I started my actual work, I only had enough time to complete half of my original goal.

What went wrong? Where had all the time gone? Had *anything* been done? Where was my accomplishment? I spent four hours working and had very little to show for it. I was frustrated and discouraged because I did not stick to my set plan for efficiency in my workday. If I could redo this day, I would have ignored the emails and immediately addressed the planned work, and both tax returns would have been reviewed instead of just one. I suddenly felt overwhelmed with regret. This frustration drove me into a whirlwind of thoughts: what if this, what if that, and so on. I felt angry at myself for not doing what I needed to do. I had no structure, and when presented with a distraction, I fell into the trap.

When I transitioned from working two full-time jobs to devoting myself to my business, I had no idea how much time I needed to spend on any task. Up until that point, I had thought of my business as a side gig, and this distorted my perception of how much of my day I spent on it. It was just some extra money, so I didn't bother to track anything. Once I left my employed position and started focusing on my business, I began to take things more seriously. I designated chunks of time for work.

Unless I was actively working, I did not sit at a desk or on my computer. Somehow, I still checked emails, responded to messages from clients, and did small tasks because "it only takes a second." I would start the day and use up a significant amount of time trying to decide what I needed to do and when I needed to do it. I had no plan, so naturally, if I had emails from anyone, I looked at them first, as this was the most tangible sign there was something that needed to be done. I would look in my customer resource management software and address any outstanding client tasks because that was the next tangible thing that I could use to decide what to do. I didn't have a structured system in place, so a lot of things fell through the cracks or weren't addressed as urgently as they should have been. Likewise, a lot of tasks that were not urgent at all were completed significantly faster than something else. All because I didn't prioritize.

In those early stages of growing the business, I planned chunks of time for childcare for my daughter, which worked out great because she was cared for, and I had the dedicated time to work on my business. However, due to my lack of planning and overall organization, I wasted a significant amount of money paying for childcare. If I had a better plan in place, I would have been more productive at a lower cost and would not have worked as much during that first full-time tax season. Often, I felt overwhelmed, uncertain, and stressed about my workload. I felt completely in the dark. I rarely felt a sense of accomplishment for any of the work that I was doing. Every day, the stress built onto the stress from the prior day.

During tax season that year, I worked more hours than ever. This realization was shocking because I thought I was working part-time! After those long months of frustration and inefficient work, I decided to make a change. Once I understood that keeping a structured schedule would help me stick to my committed work schedule, I began to work more efficiently, and stress became a small thing rather than a regular part of my life.

## WHAT IS STRUCTURED SCHEDULING?

People crave order and consistency. A structured schedule can help you better prioritize your tasks and allocate time more effectively. Clear planning helps you avoid procrastination and stress so you can achieve your goals and stay accountable for your tasks. Using a structured schedule for working time as well as personal time allows you to maintain a better work-life balance, as well as improve your time- and cognitive-management processes. A lack of structure leads to panic and chaos. Panic and chaos distort your perception of reality, causing undue stress that grows and grows.

Structured scheduling is the process of taking your allocated work time and compartmentalizing it. If you work a traditional workday, nine-to-five Monday through Friday, then 9:00 a.m. to 5:00 p.m. is your chunk of time each day allocated for work. Structured scheduling takes this allocated time and breaks it down into smaller, more manageable segments.

Let's say that you have a workday that starts at 9:00 a.m. You have a 3-hour chunk of time to work before lunch, and, in this time, you want to prepare reports for two clients, you have a previously scheduled client review session for thirty minutes at 10:00 a.m., and you want to check emails for 15 minutes before you take your lunch break. Your breakout for your three-hour work time could look like this:

- 9:00 to 10:00 a.m. priority work
- 10:00 to 10:25 a.m. new and existing client calls
- 10:30 to 11:45 a.m. priority work
- 11:45 a.m. to 12:00 p.m. check emails

Please note the new and existing client calls was set for just under 30 minutes to allow transition time.

Why should you care about time-blocking for categories of work instead of just tasks? Shouldn't there be more detail? More definition? No. And actually, you need the opposite. The goal of structured scheduling is to make your work and goals more manageable and attainable. Creating a time block for every task is overwhelming. It's your to-do list that should have all your tasks listed. Remember our goal here is to work as efficiently as possible according to our cognitive functioning. Time-blocking by category groups similar tasks together, allows for task flexibility, and eliminates unnecessary process switching.

Schedule categories are entirely up to you. Here are some of examples of categories that can be used.

- "Priority Work" covers any work that generates income directly. For me, this includes reviewing tax returns, reviewing financial statements, preparing an analysis for a client, or writing a report.
- "Admin Work" includes any work that does not generate income directly. This can be creating training videos for staff, paying bills, tracking time billing, or registering for conferences.
- "New and Existing Client Calls" consist of time chunks set aside for clients to schedule phone calls.
- "Training and Education" is dedicated to research, seminars, or anything else that enhances professional knowledge.

- "Creative Work" is work that is innovative or artistic.
- "Thinking Time" is just that. Sometimes, you need time to think and be free.
- "Space" is a category to ensure that you don't overcommit.
- "Check Emails" is a set time to check emails.
- "Weekly Planning" is time to plan out your schedule.

At the time I am writing this, my main categories are writing, priority work, and reviewing work from staff. My staff accountant is primarily working on priority work but is also focusing a lot on training. We are in the holiday season, and the IRS has closed their e-filing system for the next few weeks, so no tax returns are being filed. I am focusing more time on writing and developing new revenue streams, and she's studying for the CPA exam. In a few weeks, when tax season begins, our priorities and associated categories will change again. Your categories can change over time too. This is a fluid process.

## STRUCTURED SCHEDULING HELPS RELIEVE CHRONIC STRESS

Stress can be both positive and negative. Healthy levels of stress motivate us and drive us to action. Do you ever feel stressed for extended time periods? You can't quite tie it back to any one cause? You're just generally stressed. This negative type of stress is chronic stress. In 2018, *Everyday Health* conducted a research study showing that we have a national epidemic of chronic stress.[12] This affects both our mental health and physical health. It disrupts sleeping patterns, causes weight fluctuations, and opens us to repetitive sickness. It affects our immune systems and our moods and affects our relationships both professionally and personally. In their surveys, they found that almost a third of participants have visited a doctor about something stress-related, 57 percent claim to be paralyzed by stress, a little over a third of participants claim their work is a regular source of stress, and 47 percent claim they respond to stress by taking it out on themselves. This is a big deal if over half of everyone is stressed! Knowing this, I feel less alone and hope you do too.

What is causing all this stress for everyone? What has changed in our society? With more technology and information available to us at our fingertips, the need for in-person interaction has dwindled. According to the same *Everyday Health* article, 60 to 67 percent of young adults check social media daily, if not more often. For older adults, this is closer to 53 percent.[13] This social isolation adds to stress, creating the conflicting feelings of always being alone yet never being alone. It's what neuroscientist Dr. Stephen Porges calls the social engagement theory.[14] Per Porges, people don't always need closeness and in-person connections, but it is needed to a degree and should not be gone altogether. If we don't have face-to-face interactions, our bodies become defensive—in other words, stressed. We need each other!

Still, you can only give so much of yourself before you run out of *you* to give. Self-care may seem selfish, but taking care of yourself is not being selfish! You need to replenish the source of everything that you give so you can be the best version of yourself and serve others to your best ability.

## PERSONAL CARE INVENTORY

Both physical and mental health are key to your ability to function. Failure to include personal care in your regular schedule negatively impacts your mental, physical, and emotional health. It strains relationships, lowers your confidence and self-esteem, causes health problems, decreases productivity, and diminishes your quality of life.

Personal care is a very important element of our lives and is crucial to our overall well-being. Regular exercise, hygiene routines, getting enough sleep, and maintaining a well-balanced diet are personal care practices that are essential for staying in good physical health. Managing stress, reflection, and relaxation can help reduce or eliminate depression, stress, anxiety, and many other mental health issues. Maintaining personal and business relationships, as well as participating in activities that boost your self-esteem and confidence is key to improving your personal care. Planning personal care in your schedule ensures that work won't consume your schedule.

How do we incorporate personal care into our schedule? First, we make a Personal Care Inventory. This is what I call a list of personal care activities that are important and beneficial to an individual. Detailing the items that improve your health is imperative to determining what care activities need to be added to your schedule and how often. What you want is a well-rounded mix of personal care activities. Consider the following categories:

**Hygiene:** Any activity that refreshes you physically, such as a nice, long bath.

**Physical Health**: Moving your body like running, walking, or any other exercise.

**Spiritual Health**: Reading the Bible, prayer, meditation, and rejuvenation.

**Mental Health**: Seeing a therapist or spending time with loved ones.

**Rejuvenation**: Anything that refreshes you and takes time away from social media like reading, spending time in nature, or taking an afternoon off from electronic devices.

**Experience**: Travel, going to a concert, having a night out with friends, or shopping.

**Fun or Creative**: Writing music, working on a craft project, playing a board game.

Here are some of my personal care activities:

- A long bath alone: Hygiene—periodically
- Running/working out: Physical—a few times a week

- Prayer/read Bible: Spiritual—daily
- Lunch with colleagues: Mental—biweekly
- Reading a book: Experience—a few times a week
- Shopping: Experience—periodically
- Lunch with a friend: Experience—twice weekly
- Day at the zoo: Experience—periodically
- Recording my music: Fun/Creative—weekly
- Day without social media: Rejuvenation—weekly
- Few hours with phone turned off: Rejuvenation—weekly

Your personal care items will differ from those of someone else. For instance, I like to run long-distance in the mornings. My staff accountant, Jade, likes to do yoga with her dogs before starting her day. I find yoga uninteresting, and Jade would rather die than go for a run. Both are different exercise activities that serve the same goal: promoting better physical and mental health. Everyone is different and has unique needs.

## Action

Create a list of your personal care items and identify how often you aim to do them. This will ensure that your health and well-being are factored into your schedule.

Once you have your personal care inventory, you can create your schedule. I use structured scheduling to build out my work and personal schedule. Starting with personal care is incredibly important because entrepreneurs can so easily forget to care for themselves. The personal care inventory acts as a bank of things you can do for yourself that you can pull from as needed.

# HOW TO SET UP YOUR SCHEDULE

This is the point where cognitive management and time management intersect. We take the list of tasks we created in Chapter 2 for cognitive management and create a to-do list and a structured schedule. The goal of this exercise is to take your knowledge of how and when you best perform at certain activities and apply a time structure to that.

You can time-block your calendar in two different ways: as a placeholder or as an appointment. If you time-block as an appointment, then that solidifies the time for that specific activity. If you time-block as a placeholder, then, as more specific tasks come up, you can add additional time entries as appointments. For example, priority work time will always show as the placeholder in your calendar. If you need an hour to review a project with a client during your priority work time, you will set an appointment for this. Admin work is another one that will pretty much always show as a placeholder. You don't need to add a task entry into your calendar for every single tiny admin duty that you have.

Don't add every little task into your calendar. The client calls placeholder timeframe will have appointments scheduled in it for the specific client phone calls. As admin tasks arise, add them to your task list, not your calendar, with a reminder during your admin time to address them.

Your to-do list and your calendar should be in sync with each other, but they should not be the same. Your to-do list is more specific, with each individual task. For example, a to-do list would include tasks and activities like scheduling annual doctor checkups, reviewing XYZ client reports, researching a specific topic for ABC clients, or registering for industry conferences. Your calendar will be broader, but it will set types of tasks for certain times of day and structure them accordingly. Your calendar may have a thirty-minute slot every single day dedicated to checking emails, so you know every day, during that time, you are checking emails. Your calendar will have chunks of time dedicated to your priority work. You shouldn't have a task for checking emails because that's not very specific, and time is blocked out for this on your calendar. Likewise, you may add "wash dishes" to your task list, but you know that it can be fit in any time, and you don't need to schedule a block in your calendar for it.

Here is an example of my cognitive management list from Chapter 2:

1. Run three miles: SIMPLE—anytime

2. Review two tax returns: COMPLEX—morning

3. Review financial statements for one client: COMPLEX—morning

4. Writing a report to the IRS for a client: COMPLEX—morning

5. Three new client consult phone calls: Simple/Complex—afternoon

6. Checking emails: SIMPLE—evening (if once per day)

7. Washing the dishes: SIMPLE—evening

8. One-hour educational webinar: SIMPLE—anytime

9. Administrative tasks: SIMPLE—anytime

Here is the transformed list that will become your written to-do list:

- Prayer/Reflection
- Run three miles
- Review tax return—XYZ client
- Review tax return—UVW client
- Review financials—ABC client
- Write report—DEF client

- Training/Education—time management webinar
- Client 1 call
- Client 2 call
- Client 3 call
- Pay credit card
- Register for conference
- Send training video to assistant
- Wash dishes

Here is what you will put in your calendar:

- 9:00 a.m.-12:00 p.m.—Priority Work
- 1:00 p.m.-2:00 p.m.—Training/Education
- 2:00 p.m.-4:00 p.m.—Client Calls
- 4:00 p.m.-4:30 p.m.—Admin Time
- 4:30 p.m.-5:00 p.m.—Check Emails

Your schedule will be different from someone else's. There's no one-size-fits-all approach. I know this can seem intimidating. It's quite freeing, though. Your schedule shouldn't make you feel trapped. It should make you feel secure that you have a plan. Here are some examples of different schedules.

## MY SCHEDULE

I typically start my day with exercise because I have learned that I exercise best in the morning. I also like to start my day with prayer and reflection. I find this to be refreshing. When I start to work, I jump right in. I do not plan or check emails. I go straight to work. I think better earlier in the day and get more tired as time goes on. I save some afternoons for client calls and sometimes do some administrative work as well. I end the day by checking emails and planning my workload for the next day. I almost always address emails at the end of the day and schedule responses to be sent at the beginning of the next workday.

## VISUAL OF MY SCHEDULE

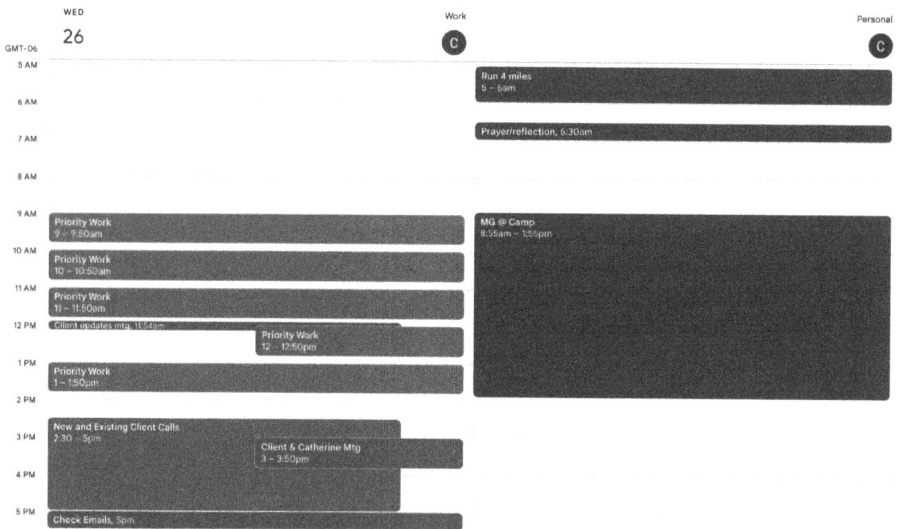

## JADE'S SCHEDULE

Jade works remotely as a staff accountant in my CPA firm. She starts her day doing yoga with her dogs. She avoids using her phone during this period. She is currently studying for a certification exam and uses her mornings to study. This works best for her because her mind is fresh, and she can focus better and retain information. After studying, she checks emails and plans her day. She takes a break and walks her dogs before starting priority work. She does all her priority work early in the afternoon and takes the evening off. She does not do any work or study after 7:00 p.m. She knows that this time is best to recuperate after a day of work and relax. She sets alarms to keep her on track with her schedule and no longer misses dinner.

## WILL'S SCHEDULE

Will, as a financial planner, structures his schedule around his priority work. He begins his day early in the morning, addressing priority work in order of importance. He can accomplish these tasks most efficiently first thing in the day because he has more analytical energy for deep thinking, and no one calls him before 8:00 a.m. He accomplishes most of the trading that needs to be done early enough to avoid last-second changes before the market closes in the afternoon. During his priority work time, he also turns email alerts off so he can focus on the work he has scheduled and not get distracted. Lunchtime and early afternoon are when he sets aside to replenish his energy and attend networking events and business lunches. In the evening, he has more productive energy again and is most creative. This is the time when he does more administrative work and creates advertisements for webinars, which is a consistent part of his work.

## EVERYONE IS DIFFERENT!

A structured schedule does not mean that you are going to operate like everyone else. As you can see from these three examples, each person has a different schedule that works for them. Will and I both focus on priority work early in the day, but Jade does her priority work early afternoon. Jade starts her day by checking emails and planning out her workload, but I do my planning and email checking at the end of the prior day. Each person also has their unique tricks to staying on schedule without interruption. Jade sets alarms, Will mutes notifications, and I schedule delayed emails. None of us came up with these techniques overnight. There was a lot of trial and error. Practice makes perfect.

## WHAT ARE YOUR FEARS?

"Wow! This is a lot of work to do. I already feel like I have no time to work on everything else that needs to be done. Is this additional work going to really benefit me when I could be doing 'real' work? Do I even have a schedule? This is a lot to take in. I've tried many other things, and none of them worked, so why should this? I really have no idea how long my work takes because I've never really tracked it before."

These are all thoughts that I had, and you may have them too. Society is pushing so much unregulated noise into your head, leading you to believe that this could be impossible. This isn't your fault! The status quo is pressuring you to hold these doubts. I promise you, though, that you are not alone in this fight.

### FEAR: THIS SEEMS LIKE TOO MUCH WORK

Progress is work. I won't deny that. If all the important things in life were easy, then everybody would do them. Why are so many people stuck in this cycle of being pulled on the clock at all hours of the day? Why do we have a chronic stress epidemic? Why are there so many frustrated entrepreneurs working all the time and facing burnout? If the status quo was working, we wouldn't have all these health issues. Making lifestyle changes and shifting your mindset is work. You will see that I am breaking all of this down into doable pieces. This process has multiple steps that you can take at your own pace. This is work, but I promise you that it's not too much work.

### FEAR: IS MY SCHEDULE TOO INCONSISTENT FOR STRUCTURED SCHEDULING?

Even the most inconsistent schedule can still be generally planned out the day before. Your scheduled time blocks don't have to be planned out far in advance or be the same on a day-to-day basis. You can make a recurring task in your calendar for anything that is consistent. It is still better to plan what you're going to do—even if you plan the day before—than to have tomorrow come and not know what's happening. Traditionally, a schedule has been treated like a bible. With less technology, there was less fluctuation in appointments. What you wrote down became the law. Nowadays you can drag an appointment from one time slot to another in an app instantly. Unless you are using a permanent pen on a notebook, you can easily adjust.

### FEAR: I'M AFRAID OF CHANGE

The most difficult aspect of structured scheduling is making the change. Change can be frustrating, especially if you're nervous about trying something new or unsure if it will even work. You may also fear that, because everything else so far has failed, this will be the same way. Living without structure is stressing you out. It stressed me out too. If you feel like I did, like nothing was ever really getting done even though you were working all the time, then the change is worth it. Just take it one day at a time. Progress will come. It doesn't happen overnight because this is always a work in progress. I promise that you will see results.

### FEAR: I DON'T KNOW HOW LONG A PARTICULAR TASK IS GOING TO TAKE

Structured scheduling isn't completely tied to your individual tasks. Block out a certain time to work on each task and allow your schedule to be flexible enough to adjust. Maybe you need to continue a task in the future, at a different time. Maybe you need to allow for your allocated time to run over if you're close to finishing a task. For example, if you know that you have a task with a deadline and you need to get that done no matter what, don't schedule a ton of client calls immediately after your scheduled priority work time. Add flexibility. If a task that you're struggling to estimate time on runs over, you can have the space and flexibility to continue working on it if needed.

**FEAR: WHAT IF I CAN'T KEEP TO MY SCHEDULE?**

Nothing works all the time. Emergencies and other inconsistencies will always pop up. Structured scheduling is designed to keep you on track and help you stick to your goals, not to lock you into a forced time frame that you otherwise would not have. For example, if you are very ill and need to go to the doctor, then clear your schedule and go to the doctor. Having the structure will help you determine how to address your workload when you have emergencies. You don't need to force yourself to stick directly to the schedule all the time. Anything can change, and that's just part of life. Go easy on yourself. The mindset change comes with practice and understanding that life happens too. This tool will help you prepare for these inconsistencies.

## WHAT DOES MY LIFE LOOK LIKE AFTER?

Looking back at the early stage of my business, I see clearly that I wasted so much time. I could have been so productive but missed so many opportunities. I needed more structure in my workday, or everything was going to fall apart. I had never created a plan for my workday before. I knew that my schedule was in such flux that I wanted to make sure that I could be flexible. I didn't realize at the time that structuring your schedule doesn't prohibit you from being flexible. Structure holds you accountable for accomplishing the goals you set. It's your responsibility to make sure that you structure your schedule to be flexible but still retain accountability.

My life has changed significantly since I brought this business full-time. Today, I have a set plan for what I'm going to do and when I'm going to do it. I always have a set time to check emails once a day in the off-season and slightly more during busy seasons. I also have allocated time for general administrative tasks and schedule planning so I know what needs to be done first and how to best approach it. At this point, I no longer start a priority work time slot by planning workload or checking emails. These two tasks have their own time slots, so I can focus on getting work done during my priority work time.

I feel a sense of pride in my work that I never felt before. Now, I end each day knowing exactly what I accomplished that day. If anything isn't completed, or I run out of time on a project, I have a plan in place for when I am going to work on it next. This creates a sense of hopefulness instead of helplessness. I can, at the end of each day, go to bed knowing that I accomplished a lot of work and know when the rest will be done. I now have the clarity to see all that I DID accomplish that day.

## Action

Get a planner or set up an online calendar that will sync to all your devices to use for your structured schedule. Planning one week should take 15 to 20 minutes.

1. Merge your task lists for cognitive management and time management. You should end up with a complexity scale, time of day, and specific time chunk for each task or activity.

2. Think about the tasks and activities that you need and want to perform over a certain time period, whether it is one day or a week.

3. For each day that you plan, create a list of the tasks and activities for that day and order them first by your cognitive management process.

4. Then, since everything can't always happen as planned, build out your specific time chunks for these activities, keeping in mind your ordered and what is feasible for your schedule.

Make it your goal to stay on schedule for the days that you just set up. Commit to trying, and I promise that you will see results. You are on the road to success!

# Chapter 4
# Communication Boundaries

Let me tell you something. Emails are the worst. I have lived every day struggling with the constant pull to get sucked into what I like to call "email infinity," the phrase that I like to use that describes what happens when I start checking emails and responding as I go. They just keep coming. From the moment that I wake up, I see the emails that have already been accumulating. I easily receive hundreds of emails every day, and I could potentially spend an entire day only checking email.

I have wasted so much time getting stuck in email infinity. New emails come in, and responses start to come in for the other emails, and then, at that point, I'm completely unable to work on the project I had designated for that day. I get trapped in the cycle of checking emails and responding to emails, and then it never ends.

How do we fix this? Emails do need to be checked but work also needs to be done. Remember your structured schedule from Chapter 3? The schedule only works if you stick to it. Setting boundaries for when and how we work is key to pulling out of the infinity loop. If emails eat into your productivity, create boundaries for yourself to only look at email at set times. If you feel confident that you can get by only checking your email once a day, then go for it. If you feel like you need to check emails five times a day, that is OK too. Plan it out and set specific times for checking emails, whether once a day or four times a day. I'm not telling you that you can't check your email during the day all day long, but you also can't sit there checking your email throughout your priority work time.

## EMAILS STEAL YOUR TIME AND ENERGY

Approximately 333 billion emails were sent and received around the world daily in 2022 alone.[15] Nearly 57 percent of those emails were identified as spam.[16] Almost 47 percent of all emails came from bots that same year.[17] If your inbox looks like mine, it is slammed by advertisements and demands for meetings from spammers. Unfortunately, only around 14.3 percent of emails are caught by spam filters.[18] How does this affect workplace productivity? A never-ending influx of emails creates constant notifications, nagging you to look at them. These interruptions lead to "context switching," the process when you switch back and forth between working on tasks and checking your emails.[19] This constant back and forth can make you more prone to errors and less productive in your work.

Psychology professors and experts Gloria Mark, Daniela Gudith, and Ulrich Klocke conducted a study on the effect of interruptions on work tasks.[20] Their goal was to see whether the type of interruptions mattered, how the interruptions affected the time for task completion, and the overall differences between responses from the individuals. They found that when people completed interrupted tasks, they incurred much higher stress levels, effort involved, and frustration overall. People with more open-minded personality traits responded better to interruptions. However, people who need more personal structure did not adapt as quickly. In our current society, everyone wants faster. According to this study, faster is not better and leads to greater levels of stress and workload frustration. Working under these conditions should never be long-term and absolutely should never be a part of our everyday lifestyle.

Psychology researchers Gloria Mark, Shamsi T. Iqbal, Mary Czerwinski, Paul Johns, and Akane Sano conducted a study specifically reviewing the impact of email usage patterns on stress and productivity in the workplace.[21] They collected data from 40 participants and determined that approximately 4.5 hours were spent on average, daily, on the computer, of which almost 90 minutes were spent on email. The research participants checked their email an average of 77 times a day, motivated both by external notifications and self-driven checks. Their study showed that greater time spent on email negatively impacted the individuals' productivity and increased their stress levels. They also found that individuals who checked email on their own initiative were more productive than the individuals who checked emails primarily because they received notifications. Overall, productivity and the individuals' mental well-being decreased with more time spent on emails.

Many people check emails as one of the first, if not the very first, tasks of their workday and then proceed to spend a large portion of their work time checking emails, sometimes several times within the same hour. Most of the emails received aren't even high-priority emails that need more timely responses. Most of them are either scams, promotions, newsletters, or other subscriptions. All this time spent checking emails can lead to missed deadlines, longer work hours, and increased stress levels.

## INBOX SESSION VERSUS QUICK SKIM

I have two different methods of checking emails: the inbox session and the quick skim. The inbox session is the one time each day that I do a full review of all emails. I schedule this as the last task of the day before planning my work for the next day. My goal is to review each email and determine if I should create a task and set a date for it to be addressed, if I should respond to it quickly in three minutes or less, or if I just need to delete it. This way, I can continue moving forward and check all the emails without stopping and jumping between different items. When the next day starts, I already know what I will work on. Depending on how busy we are and what projects we are working on, I may check my email more than once per day, but it is always scheduled. Planning is key.

The quick skim is more difficult to master than the inbox session. If you are in a busy season, facing deadlines, or expect urgent emails, the quick skim can help you check your emails for the important ones first.

1. Open your email and set a timer for a short period of time, like five or ten minutes. The timer is very important to set a limit for yourself and avoid email infinity.

2. During this time, skim your unread emails to determine their importance. Ignore ads and spam and leave them for the inbox session. Briefly review the remaining emails to determine if they can wait for the inbox session or if they need to be addressed.

Here's an example of a quick skim session: One day, I opened my email and saw ten new emails. Two were advertisements, two were newsletters, three were spam, two were client responses to project questions, and one was a response from a referral partner responding to my meeting request for the next day. Of all these items, the referral partner's email was the one that needed to be addressed right away. I responded to him that noon worked. Sending a response during the day was necessary. Waiting until my inbox session in the evening would not have been appropriate in this case. All other emails were fine to wait until the evening.

By setting boundaries with how I review and address emails, I ensure that I am committed to how I spend my time with each activity and what gets done. If I have a set time to check emails, then that is all I do. If I have a set time to do work on projects, I immediately begin the project without unnecessarily opening emails and starting everything over fresh. This breaks me out of email infinity and moves me forward into focusing on actual work and being productive.

*Action*

Now, I want you to pull out your calendar and schedule a time to check your emails. Choose times that work best for you and commit to them. Don't beat yourself up if you don't stick to the times. This is a learning process. If you discover that you can't stick to the times you chose, try new times. These changes are all a work in process.

## BOUNDARIES GONE WRONG

Do you ever find yourself in situations where clients disregard your boundaries? Do you ever ignore your own boundaries when clients push you? I have a few examples of times when boundaries with clients went way wrong.

## CLIENT WANTED MY FRIDAY AFTERNOONS

A potential client contacted me looking for some accounting and tax services for multiple entities. After reviewing her email detailing her needs, I responded to her with a link to my scheduler so we could meet to discuss further. She replied, "My only availabilities are on Friday afternoons. Let me know if that is an option." I wanted to help her out because she was a referral from a close friend, so I suggested a date I could fit her in. I don't typically schedule client meetings on Fridays. That time is set aside for other tasks. She thanked me and responded that she was only available after 2:30 p.m.

Once she realized that I was accommodating what I perceived as a one-time situation, she explained, "My availability will remain limited to Friday afternoons, so unless that is a temporary lack of availability for client support on Friday afternoons, this might not be a great fit."

Without hesitation, I replied to her email, thanking her for her honesty, and agreed with her that we would not be the best fit for her and wished her the best of luck. She appreciated this candor and thanked me again.

Did I land a new client? No. Did I lock myself into forced work late every Friday afternoon? Also, no. Do I have any regrets? Absolutely not.

## SUNDAY BEFORE DEADLINE PANIC

A new client reached out to me to prepare a tax return due a month later. Usually, at this stage in the game, most accountants are nonresponsive to new leads. We had some availability, so I told her we could do our best to try to get it done by the deadline but made no promises. She then signed our contract, which clearly states that she had already missed the deadline for timely filing. There were no surprises.

Five days before the tax deadline, she sent a message confirming she had sent us all the information so we could begin her tax return. Luckily, we were available to start it right away and completed the return draft on Friday, three days before the deadline. Our admin team sent the draft for approval Sunday morning. This was one of two last-minute returns that we already knew may or may not get out in time. Up until this point, we generally try to avoid actively working on projects that are due within 48 hours.

I received a message from the client in my portal Sunday morning asking if they could schedule a call that same day to discuss the tax return. Next, they called three times and sent two text messages. A few hours later, they disapproved the document in the system and sent an email detailing all the changes they believed were necessary. They sent another email stating that they had texted, called, and chatted, that the return was incorrect and that they were concerned.

I connected with the client on Monday, the next day, to review their return and found that they didn't send everything needed. Not once did she apologize for her and her husband's behavior the prior day. I informed them that they had an extension on their return and her response was, "If I had known there was an extension, I would not have been blowing up your phone yesterday. I am not this crazy of a person."

I could tell that she was embarrassed by the situation but clearly justified it. The justification told me she could very possibly do the same thing in the future.

## LABOR DAY INVOICE QUESTIONS

I prepared a tax return for a business and sent their final bill, signature pages, and client copy after they approved the draft on the Friday before Labor Day. This client had taken their accounting function in-house, so the books were completed by their office assistant. An office assistant should not be maintaining the accounting for a business, so they ended up with messy books that required extensive review and corrections.

On Saturday morning over the holiday weekend, the client sent a message through our portal asking questions. He sent me another message the next working day before hours, asking the same questions again. When I did not answer either message by 6:00 a.m. on Tuesday after Labor Day, he reached out to my staff accountant, Jade. He then asked her his questions about the bill, stating that he had been unable to get a response from me. This was all over the course of a holiday weekend. This tax return was not even due for another ten days. Even if it were due the next week, there was no reason that he needed to demand an answer regarding a bill over a holiday weekend. It's OK that he sent the messages, but he should not have had the expectation that they would have been answered prior to the next workday.

In this situation, Jade and I both reacted correctly by responding to the client's inquiries on the next workday, as should have been expected. We both reiterated to the client that we were not in the office at the time that he sent questions and responded once we were available and working.

## WHAT WENT WRONG IN THESE SITUATIONS?

Clients shouldn't expect us to be available late Friday afternoons, over weekends, or on holidays. Receiving overwhelming messages and calls on Monday is very intense and stressful. Clients' expectations that they will receive answers to same-day questions on a Sunday is not OK with me. I don't run the kind of business that is willing to provide that level of involvement.

From these experiences, I learned that, while I do have detailed client expectations with regard to when information is needed, I need to better clarify my expectations for the days leading up to a deadline. Since I don't always work directly with clients during the 48 hours before their tax deadlines, I need to make that part of my written procedures for clients. If I had communicated boundaries to these clients, I may have avoided the latter two situations altogether.

## BOUNDARIES DEFINE YOU

According to psychologists Dr. Henry Cloud and Dr. John Townsend, your boundaries define you.[22] They define the line between where you end and where someone or something else begins. This shows you where your self-ownership lies and what you should take responsibility for. What do you consist of? Where is that limit? Once you decide how far out you extend for any given situation, you have found your boundary. Boundaries can be physical, mental, emotional, or spiritual. The boundaries we are looking at here are primarily mental and emotional in terms of setting limits for work in your business.

Work boundaries are the limits and guidelines with which you establish your relationship with work. You need to set limits for others and for yourself. The biggest boundaries to consider regarding your professional life are those involving time, communication, and overall well-being. Defining your working hours, incorporating breaks and lunch as well as personal care, and ensuring vacation time is separate from work are very important to time boundaries. These are created when you form your structured schedule. Communication boundaries and client expectations are also incredibly important. Determining your limits with regards to email and communication, remote work, and use of technology. These boundaries affect you just as much as your client. Knowing when to unplug from electronic devices and learning when to say no are important skills to develop.

Are there times that you want to set aside to completely unplug? Do you have a definitive line between at work and at home if you work remotely? Do you have limits on whether you accept text messages from clients or if you check emails after a certain hour? Do you have a set work time when you take client calls? Do you have a plan in place for when you realize that you overcommitted or took on too much work? These are all examples of questions to determine if there is a boundary that you need to establish.

---

## Action

Start a list of potential boundaries that you need to put in place for yourself and a list for your clients. This will take some time because you're not going to think of everything upfront. With a list you can add to it as something comes to you. Here is an example list:

- Email response time
- Eliminate business text messages
- No phone during priority work
- No work on Sundays
- No same day meetings
- No new projects five days before a deadline

---

## HOW TO SET BOUNDARIES

There are four actions that need to be taken to have successful boundaries: define, establish, communicate, and enforce.

1. **Define.** Defining your boundaries involves taking time to reflect and consider your values, needs, and comfort in various situations. This is your list of boundaries.

2. **Establish.** The next step is to establish a boundary for yourself. Commit to the stance that you don't schedule meetings the same day under ordinary circumstances.

3. **Communicate.** Then, communicate this to the client or another outside person. Setting a boundary and letting a client know that you don't do meetings on the same day isn't rude. You can communicate the boundary in many different positive ways. One method would be to let the client know that you don't typically have availability within a certain time frame and suggest other times to schedule the meeting.

4. **Enforce.** Once you have communicated this boundary, you need to enforce it. This is the toughest part! You must hold firm to your boundaries. Most people don't hold to their boundaries because they haven't established or communicated them. Communicating your boundary commits you to it and lessens your chance of backing off.

## MY COMMUNICATIONS EXPECTATIONS

My business has many different expectations, such as how quickly phone calls and emails are returned, how and when we schedule client meetings and phone calls, the deadlines for submitting documentation, and how we receive client information.

We have one policy in place where, generally, calls and emails will be answered within two working days. Both calls and emails will always receive some kind of receipt. This is important because it confirms to our clients that we have received their message. A response confirming receipt of an email is still better than no response at all. If clients call with specific questions or leave a message that they have questions, we respond to that call via email requesting send their questions via email so that we can prepare a response and schedule a call efficiently. We set hours of availability at specific times for client meetings and phone calls. We generally do not have client meetings on the weekends, whether we are working or not. Clients should expect that if they need a meeting, it should be scheduled in advance and within our working hours.

## MEGAN'S COMMUNICATION EXPECTATIONS

Email correspondence is used today as another means to chat or send instant messages. Megan has learned in her coaching business that if someone sends an email with what they claim is an "easy question," and she replies, then she has set an unspoken standard of instant access. By providing the individual with a fast, back-and-forth texting style response, the individual will see that she is available and open to responding back and forth over email. To counter this, she intentionally waits to reply to emails, even if she has seen the email already. By responding later, whether it's an hour later or a day later, she sends the expectation that she is going to respond in a timely manner but not instantaneously. If a conversation is needed, then she can request a meeting with the client.

Megan wants her clients to understand that they don't need to come to her with everything. In her onboarding process, she assigns a team member to be that client's dedicated consultant. She explains to the client that the dedicated team member will always respond faster than her, so they know what to expect.

Often, a client will still email Megan questions that her team has the capacity to answer in a much more cost-effective and time-efficient manner. In these situations, she will reply and copy one of her team members, asking them to handle the request from the client. This helps the client understand that Megan is not the only person who can help but she is still addressing the question and assuring the client that the matter will be handled.

## MY OPERATIONS EXPECTATIONS

Our engagement letters detail expectations for deadlines, especially those for tax returns. We provide our own firm-specific deadlines for when we need information sent to us, when returns need to be completed, and when signatures are needed prior to deadlines. This is important because we have an internal policy stating that we don't actively work on returns two days before a deadline.

Regarding meeting structure, we never plan working sessions in person unless we need to be on-site for something at the client's location. Usually, if we meet with a client in person, it is more of a social networking type meeting than an initial consult or actual work session. While we primarily operate our business locally and maintain local office space, we work in a remote, online-based capacity. We explain to our clients in detail how documents are submitted to us since we work in a virtual environment.

## PERSONAL PHONE—BLURRED LINES OF COMMUNICATION

I have made the mistake before of giving clients my personal cell number. Most often, though, clients received my cell number from someone who referred them to me, most likely a friend who does not have my work number. These situations are unavoidable, but it is very important to set expectations right away.

One time, I received a client referral from a friend who gave my cell phone number to the prospective client. I didn't bother to distinguish between the business line and my personal phone number, and I communicated with him here and there, using both numbers from time to time. I hoped that he would understand that if I used the business number more, he would begin to use that one, but that didn't happen.

We got to a place where he would text me on my personal cell, and I would respond via the business line. At that point, everything was so confusing because I couldn't go back to any one single source for information. If I wanted to know what questions he had, then I had to look at my personal cell phone history to see what he needed. If I wanted to know what my responses were to him and how I handled his requests, then I had to go to another app for the business phone. It became very messy and ultimately led to the client calling and texting me on both numbers back-to-back if I didn't answer one or the other.

## SET CLIENT EXPECTATIONS

I have learned that, instead of accepting that the client has my cell number and communicating with them through it, I should respond to the initial text message or phone call to set up a consult but also make it very clear that this is not my professional phone number and provide the new number. I have failed to do this in the past because I don't want to hurt anyone's feelings, but giving someone the correct number to use works out better for everyone in the long run. Boundaries are useless unless you communicate them. You can decide that you are going to adhere to a boundary that you have set up for your work, but your clients aren't going to know that you have these boundaries unless you explicitly inform them.

## SOLUTIONS FOR EMAIL AND PHONE BOUNDARIES

Email communication boundaries are broad and generally apply to anyone who tries to communicate with you. Because email has a large influence on your work efficiency and time management, information regarding your communication boundaries can be included in your email signature. This is important because it immediately notifies anyone who has sent you an email about your communication protocol and procedures. If your signature indicates that emails are typically answered within two business days, then anyone you communicate with will be privy to this knowledge and can respond accordingly. Automatic email responses can also reflect your communication boundaries while confirming receipt of the message and setting an expectation for when a response will be sent. Automatic emails can be sent 24/7 to indicate response times, outside business hours to indicate that you are off the clock, or during vacation times so clients know that you are out of the office and can expect a delayed response. These automatic messages can also refer clients to another individual if someone is available and can respond faster than you.

Phone communication boundaries can be provided in the same manner as email boundaries. I strongly recommend implementing a separate business phone system, and I discourage providing your personal cell phone number to clients. You may think that providing your cell phone number seems accommodating, but this will always come back to haunt you.

As an alternative, provide clients with your business line and your direct extension. This is just as personal and does not blur the work and personal boundary lines of communication. Most phone systems will allow automatic responses to phone communication. A phone system should allow you to set up a professional voicemail to route your callers and send away messages. Away messages are used for vacations or when your business is closed. You can set up your phone system to direct callers to your main voicemail during work hours and to an away voicemail when you're closed or when you are on vacation. You can also set up your phone system to send a text response to anyone who calls without leaving a voicemail.

## DISRESPECTED TIME

Ann, a close friend of mine and fellow CPA firm owner, received a client email twenty minutes before their scheduled 4:00 p.m. appointment that read: "I'm running a little behind. Can we do 6:00 instead?" The client is a hairdresser, and her last client ran over the expected time. To be accommodating, Ann agreed to the new time.

Shortly after she arrived, the client texted, "I'm cleaning up my mess at the salon and then heading there, so it might be ten after six before I get there."

Ann responded, "I am here already. This is after hours, and I made allowance for my time, and my time is valuable. I have already made concessions, and I feel very disrespected."

The client continued, "I understand. I'm sorry. I didn't mean anything. I'm almost there if you're still there. I wish I could tell my hair clients that it's 6:00 p.m. It doesn't matter that I'm not finished and your appointment ran over, but I have to get off work. Unfortunately, I can't do that."

Emergencies can happen to anyone. In this instance, though, the client clearly did not value Ann's time and effort. If she had, she would have rescheduled immediately instead of wasting Ann's entire evening. She also would have apologized for the last-minute changes and taken ownership of her scheduling issues. Ann was already there. Waiting. She was very upset. She gave an inch, and the client took a mile.

## WHAT IS AN EMERGENCY?

An emergency looks different for every industry. An emergency for a therapist could be a client with a mental breakdown. That is an example of a true medical emergency. Short of that, very few things, if any, constitute an emergency that requires an action from you at any given point in your business. Even if you are a therapist who could have a true emergency with a client, you shouldn't be on call 24/7 for your business. Directing your clients to resources outside of your professional hours is necessary for you to be able to take a break from working. You can have a voicemail directing emergencies to the ER, or you could have an after-hours service that handles any emergencies. This is just an example of an actual emergency. Usually, when clients say they have an emergency, it's not a true emergency. In my world of accounting services, there is never a true emergency. I hear people in my industry remind each other all the time that a lack of planning on your part does not constitute an emergency on mine. You are going to have to determine what an emergency looks like for you and your business. I have decided that there are no emergencies in my business.

## WHAT HAPPENS WHEN YOU CAVE TO A CLIENT'S PERCEIVED EMERGENCY?

I have had clients tell me that they have an emergency. The emergency is that life got away from them, and they completely forgot about their tax return. The tax return wasn't important months ago when I first started asking for information, and it wasn't important at any of the three times I sent follow-up emails, all but begging for this information. For most of the year, I cared more about this client's tax return than they did.

Everyone must decide what their priorities are. Sometimes, life happens, and something like a tax return may fall on the back burner. I'm not trying to criticize people who must put something like that last on their priority list because something more important or urgent has come up. The problem is when someone has put something off for so long and, suddenly, it's due, and they decide that it is an emergency. How do you handle that? You must set your limits for how far you are willing to go for a client. If you have the availability the week before a deadline, do you push to get the work done? In the past, I would say absolutely. If I have the time available, then I should get this done for the client. However, when you cave into a client's perceived emergency, you run the risk of producing rushed, inadequate, and potentially flawed work. In your attempt to satisfy your client, you have compromised yourself and your work product.

## TRAIN AND REMIND YOUR CLIENTS

You may feel awkward about training your clients or instructing them to follow your protocols. You may worry that your clients won't understand and will struggle to follow your communication standards. The reality is that some people will take longer to grasp new concepts, especially if this is something you have not implemented before. People don't always adapt easily to change. This is why it is incredibly important to let them know what they should expect from you by giving clear and concise instructions.

You may also worry that some clients will dislike your new changes. This may very well be the case. People don't like change. Some people may become resistant to your new communication standards, but eventually, most of them will understand over time and adapt accordingly. Most people respond when they are given explicit instructions and clearly informed of what they can expect from you. There may be some clients that disregard your standards, and that's OK. In the long run, do you really want to work with someone who doesn't respect your boundaries?

## CONSISTENCY IS KEY

Consistency is the key to ensuring that your clients learn and adhere to your expectations. If you decide that you want to operate your business one way, make it happen. Don't let something happen just this one time; it sets a precedent. If you waver and say that you'll just send this email just this time and that it's a one-time thing, you are sending a message to your client that it's OK to reach out to you after hours. You're sending them the message that you sometimes work during those hours. You need to adhere to your boundaries consistently.

Setting and maintaining boundaries for the first time can feel uncomfortable and intimidating. Over time, this will seem more natural and comfortable. In the meantime, be sure to track your behavior to ensure that you are holding to your boundaries. Always hold yourself accountable first, especially before clients. You shouldn't expect anyone else to do something you aren't consistently doing, either.

Don't be afraid to follow through with the consequences of the boundaries you've set. If you tell a client that you need information by a certain date to complete a project, when that date comes and goes, don't hesitate to let them experience the consequences. Their failure to meet a deadline doesn't require you to overwork and overwhelm yourself. Practice being assertive so you can communicate your boundaries effectively, efficiently, and kindly. There is a polite way to say anything.

Finally, be patient. Developing and maintaining boundaries is quite a challenge. Changes aren't always made overnight. Be persistent with your boundaries, but have some grace for both your clients and yourself as you develop this new lifestyle.

# Chapter 5
# Management Tools and Automation

Utilizing management tools helps you stick to your structured schedule. Various tools that create structure and guidance will support your task management process, keeping you accountable and organized. At a minimum, you will need customer resource management (CRM) software, time-tracking software, and a cloud computing and productivity software package. Beyond these basics, artificial intelligence and automation for recurring work can fine-tune your efficiencies. Using these techniques to stay on track helps you use your time more efficiently and be more productive.

## CRM SOFTWARE

In my first year of business, I didn't use CRM software. I primarily relied upon the online drive of my email service provider to share and store customer files. Every time I onboarded a new client, I would create a new folder within my drive and share it with the client. Whenever I sent out a new contract, I would send a PDF that I updated manually with the client's information through an e-signature service and a questionnaire the client might or might not ignore. This was a very time-intensive manual process, and I had not even started doing actual billable work for the client. After I completed a project for a client, I would add everything to the client folder and create a bill.

All this administrative work accounted for 45 minutes to an hour of time. I had 11 clients in my first year of business. This accounted for approximately one eight-hour day, so it didn't seem like that big of a deal at the time. My business grew drastically in the second year to a total of 93 clients. At some point, early in the second year, I realized that I was being too cost-conservative. I was in denial about the tools I needed to be successful. I was still in this startup mindset, trying to keep expenses low, even if the cost was my time. Eventually, I researched various CRM programs and chose one that fit my style and needs.

The software I use now automates almost all the administrative work I was previously doing manually. If I add a client file to a particular work process, the software will send out the contract, the questionnaire in digital format, and the invoice. By incorporating this tool, I saved up to an hour of my time per client. In that second year alone, I eliminated two work weeks of administrative tasks. Customer resource management software will significantly reduce your overall administrative tasks in your business and streamline your work processes with your clients. Take the time to demo different software programs and ask questions to learn how they work so you can find the best fit for you and your organization.

## TIME-TRACKING

For most of the time I have been in business, I have only tracked billable time. In my business, I bill hourly for some projects and fixed amounts for other projects. Then, I started tracking all the hours I worked, including the administrative hours, so that I could truly understand how much time I was putting into this business. Midway through each year, I reviewed the projects I bill flat rates for and compared the cost of work performed based on hours against revenue received. One year, I found that we weren't even breaking even on the cost of labor involved for three of our recurring fixed-rate clients. I adjusted the billing for all these clients to accommodate the additional workload required. If I had not been tracking my hours for these fixed-rate engagements, then I would have had no idea we were losing money.

Since I started tracking all the hours that I work, regardless of whether they are billable or not, I have found that I perform a significant number of administrative tasks for the firm. Analyzing the time that I spend on some of these tasks can come in handy when trying to decide if this work is being done efficiently or if it's keeping me from working on revenue-generating projects.

Tracking hours that are billed hourly is very important so you can properly determine the time spent on the project and bill accordingly. However, not all the work that you do is going to be work that is billed hourly. You'll always have administrative work that you can't bill for. You may also charge flat rates in addition to or in lieu of hourly billing. Charging your client and getting your work done can happen for those tasks without tracking billing, but doing so will prevent you from collecting valuable efficiency data. You must track your time and analyze the cost of your services against the revenue those services bring in. Tracking time for all types of work will help you see where your practice is efficient and where improvements can be made.

## CLOUD COMPUTING AND PRODUCTIVITY SOFTWARE PACKAGES

Many major providers of email services and domain management bundle other cloud computing and productivity software functions into their packages. Most include email, calendar, task list, cloud drive, video conference, team chat, and workspace, among many other functions. All these services can potentially come bundled with your email service. I use all these services and more that are available from my provider. It's very likely you have available resources that are either free or already included in a package you are already using.

My email provider includes a calendar that I use to schedule my meetings and appointments, both business and personal, as well as my structured schedule time blocks. It includes a video conference feature that I use for virtual meetings. It has a team chat, workspace, and cloud drive functions so we can message and share information. There is a task list function that I use to create tasks and assign days for them. Having a major provider encompassing all these tools allows you to integrate all these functions for a seamless workflow. My team enjoys these features because we can all be on the same page effortlessly.

## REINVENT THE TO-DO LIST

The traditional, never-ending to-do list is counterproductive to your success. An infinite list of all the things you need to do is overwhelming and stressful and can lead to you never feeling accomplished. Instead, create a well-defined task list with deadlines. Deadlines keep you focused and show you that an end is insight. I use the task list function from my email service provider. This is a glorified to-do list in the cloud. The key difference between this and a traditional to-do list is that I can assign dates and times to each item on the list. Assigning dates or deadlines to tasks helps you plan for them and make sure that they are being completed. I know that if I have something on a to-do list, I may or may not look at it today. If it's on a to-do list and assigned to me today, I will make sure I address it.

1. When I create a new task, I always add details that will help me remember more quickly what I need to do to get started, and I always assign a date to the task.

2. At the beginning of each day, I review my task list for what I have scheduled that day and work accordingly.

**3.** When my workday ends, either everything for that day has been checked off and completed, or I can reevaluate the remaining tasks and allocate them to a future date.

Checking off tasks and watching them disappear as they are completed provides me with a sense of accomplishment and success. Allocating tasks I was unable to complete to future dates allows me to feel secure and relieved that, although I did not get everything done today, I have a plan and a set date to review that task in the future. Revising the to-do list process will help you make progress in your work and keep moving forward efficiently.

This to-do list can be done in many ways. One method is to use a literal to-do list either through an app or on paper, assign deadlines, and check each item off when completed like I just described. However, there are other approaches that can be used once you have mastered the basics. I have realized that my to-do lists primarily center around emails. One method of task organization is to use a folder system for email management, along with labels and color-coding. You may find that a combination of this works for you or you may develop a new, unique system altogether.

## Action

Take some time and evaluate where you may need a management tool that can help you complete or automate a manual process. Look at your current email and other software providers to see what tools they offer that you can incorporate into your workflow. Evaluate your current client management processes and see where you can improve and if you need to add or change your CRM software. Write out a list of processes you may be doing that are very labor intensive and start doing research on each of them to see where you may find new efficiencies.

> Here is my list of inefficiencies and potential solutions I am exploring:
>
> - Staff aren't held accountable for time spent on fixed-rate projects.
>
>   SOLUTION: Adjust settings in time entry software to allow them more visibility.
>
> - We have too many different staff communication tools.
>
>   SOLUTION: Begin using the functions provided in the bundled package from the email provider and eliminate the need for other third-party applications.

## ARTIFICIAL INTELLIGENCE

Artificial intelligence (AI) streamlines a variety of work processes. While these tools don't replace human responsibility and decision-making, they can be very helpful in the work process. There is software for language processing that is primarily chat-driven and can compile and provide a wide array of information from the internet for your specific request. AI can be used in both your technical and administrative work. Administrative work can be aided by tools for email drafting, legal research and report drafting, marketing and SEO analysis, HR tools, video analysis, and note-takers. Technical work can be enhanced by tools that are designed specifically for your industry and help with efficiencies related to your specific work product.

In my case, I use specifically crafted financial analysis software to pull out data from financial reports to assist with my analysis for my clients, as well as tax research software that finds potential solutions to my research cases. By using software that anticipates and calculates various ratios and performs different analyses on financial statements, I am cutting down on the time I would have to take to use a spreadsheet, craft these formulas, and plug everything in from the financial statements. While I still need to double-check the math and make sure everything is accurate, I have already saved a ton of time on the data entry aspect and can now focus on the review and analysis portion of my work. Likewise, the tax research software also cuts down on the time I would have spent on the hunt for information. I am constantly hearing from tax professionals that their number-one search function when tackling a complex situation is their search engine. They type the problem into the search engine and see what comes up. The problem with this is that all the information coming in is from the internet, whether accurate or not. In my software, I can see what the sources of information are, and I can decide if I want to include that source or exclude it based on the merit I determine for that source.

When using artificial intelligence, make sure that you are checking your work and revising accordingly because none of these tools are perfect by any means and should not be taken at face value. They should merely be used as tools to help you along your journey toward your finished product. Sometimes, I use a chat program to help draft emails, and I always revise the emails to make them seem less robotic and more personal because the chat software doesn't add human flourishes to the messages. Your email recipients want to receive something that reflects you and who you are in your response. For example, my chat function always signs off on messages with best regards. I don't particularly like that, so that's one thing that I always change, but there are other small things that need to be changed in a message from the chat that make it seem inhuman.

As AI tools become more acceptable and commonplace, this will be something that people look out for. You don't want someone to look at your email and be offended that it came from AI.

## AUTOMATIONS AND RECURRING TRANSACTIONS

Manually working on recurring transactions can often be redundant and take away from time you could spend on other tasks. How do you know if a task is recurring and can be automated? Now that you have working task lists, you have a starting place to perform a task analysis. If you have a list of tasks that you typically perform on a regular basis, you can review each item and determine whether it repeats or not. If a task is repeated regularly, there may be potential for automation. Tasks that are good for automation are usually frequent, relatively simple, generally time-consuming, and easy to integrate with other processes. Tasks that are complex or are highly involved are better not being automated. Chances are, if a task is a lot of work but easy, then it's probably something that can be automated.

## WHERE CAN I IMPROVE?

A few years back, when I was working as a solopreneur, my business was primarily a tax preparation firm that did some light annual accounting to clean up the books for the tax preparation process. At one point, I gained five regular bookkeeping clients. Looking back at my revenue stream, I see that no single month that year was consistent in bookkeeping revenue. I was performing regular work for five different clients, but I wasn't being paid consistently. Every month, I would do my billing and then wait for the client to pay the invoice. They were all very busy entrepreneurs, so I can understand that clicking on the bill and paying it was one more task that they had to add to their plate. They wanted to pay their bills, but it was just something that got put off.

Halfway through that year, I realized that I was spending so much time sending bills and chasing money that I was always stressed about what needed to be collected and what I could start working on or who I needed to stop working on because they didn't pay their bill in two months. I wasn't focusing on the work exclusively. I started researching online for solutions because I had a need. I needed some way to take these administrative tasks off my plate so that I could focus on doing the work and building more business.

I found that I could collect authorization and payment information up front from my clients and set up recurring invoices and payments for them in my software. I spent some time compiling this information and corresponding back and forth with the client to get everything I needed, but once I had it, I could set each client up for recurring billing and payment and never have to worry about that again. I could focus on the work and not the administrative task that was overwhelming me.

There is no cookie-cutter answer for any problem or need, but I can help you understand the thought processes that have helped me determine where my needs are. In this situation, I was stressed out. I knew that there was some aspect of my work that I did not like. This was my pain point. "Everything would be easier if only I didn't have to chase these clients for payments. I'm running out of time to work on these clients' bookkeeping accounts because I am spending so much time on creating invoices. I feel panicked every time I review my accounts receivable to see who I need to hound for payment for the millionth time." These thoughts led me to my search for something better. Look for your pain points. They will lead you to an improvement need.

## LIST OF MY PAIN POINTS AND POSSIBLE SOLUTIONS

- Pain: I spend a lot of time responding to clients that all have the same questions.

  SOLUTION: Create an FAQ page on the website.

- Pain: I struggle with consistency in my blog and newsletter because of the time it takes to gather content.

  SOLUTION: Use a generative AI tool to create content from reputable sources.

## Action

Is there a task you are performing in your business that you would love to remove? What do you wish for to make things easier? Do you have any recurring transactions and tasks that you perform that could potentially be automated? Make a list of what these pain points look like for you and tackle a few of them, one at a time, to see what possibilities exist for you.

# Chapter 6
# Multitasking

My mom called me one evening around 7:00 and said, "I have some great news, but I really want you to listen because you never hear what I am saying on the phone because you are always doing something else."

This upset me, and I snapped back defensively, "Of course, I'm listening!" but I realized that it was true. My work schedule is not the same as hers, so there are times that we call each other when the other is busy. As a schoolteacher, her schedule is set by the school hours, whereas my schedule is less traditional. It's very possible that, depending on the day, I could have been working at the time or even doing something else. She tells me that she can sense me going in and out of the conversation, never grasping the full context and periodically falling lost in silence.

I have discovered that if I am working on something while on the phone, it will take significantly longer for me to finish what I am doing. For example, if I am writing an email and talking on the phone, it will take about twice as long to get the email written. Sometimes, though, I will completely zone out of the call because I'll turn more focus toward the email and completely lose any focus on the phone call, forgetting entirely what we were even talking about.

I can see other ways that I zone out too. If I try to watch a webinar for training and do some work on the side, my mind ultimately shifts to the work and ignores the webinar. I have never been able to stay focused on a webinar and do work at the same time. This isn't news to me, yet I still tell myself that I can do it. I have tried to watch training sessions and check emails, complete projects, or even cook dinner at the same time. Every time, I find myself rewatching several parts over and over because I missed something. By the end, I still couldn't tell you what the main points were. And an hour-long webinar isn't an hour-long webinar if you rewind it constantly. It becomes more like two or three hours. Where's the efficiency in that?

I attended an accounting continuing education seminar once in a large lecture hall at a college. Most attendees were sitting at their desks, focused on the presentation. One lady set up a card table and chair in one of the aisles of the auditorium. She had a box full of client receipts and was sorting them on the card table. She was working, not paying attention at all to the discussion. She cheated herself out of the training and was very rude to other attendees. One hundred people could see her sitting in the middle of the room, sorting receipts.

These three examples have a lot in common. They all show how multiple tasks cannot be completed at the exact same time. They also show that focus naturally shifts to the more complex task. Our minds know when something requires more effort than it's being given. Multitasking is not efficient. It leads to stress, missed information, and a bad reputation. It leads to arguments and hurt relationships. To be more efficient and stop wasting time, it's best to focus on one thing at a time.

Multitasking prevents productivity. The term multitasking refers to either working on two or more tasks simultaneously or quickly transitioning between two or more tasks. There is a common misconception that multitasking helps you become more efficient and complete more in a shorter period. The reality is that switching back and forth between tasks, especially high-level tasks, causes you to process and perform at a much lower speed than if you work through each task to completion before moving to the next one. Multitasking also leads to a greater number of errors in your work product. I can tell that I feel more drained and less accomplished when I try to juggle multiple tasks. I also get stuck doing a lot of rework to accommodate for sloppy work.

Essentially, your brain does three things when facing a task: absorb info, decide how to handle it, and perform an action. The first stage is *identifying the stimulus*. This is where the brain receives information from your senses and stores this information in your working memory. The second stage is *deciding a response*. In this stage, the brain takes the stored information and decides to act upon it. Then, the third stage is *action taking*, where your brain performs the action decided based on the stored memory. There is some significant work involved here. Your brain follows this process every single time you change a task, from working on a project to walking.[23]

This process is faster for simple tasks and takes longer for more complex tasks. It's easy to put a dish in the dishwasher, stir a pot on the stove, and then go back to putting dishes in the dishwasher. These are easy things to switch back and forth between. It takes much longer to switch back to working on a report for a client when you pause to check and respond to emails from other clients. These are more complex tasks than simple housework and require more time in the cognitive process.[24]

When your brain transitions between tasks, it follows another cognitive process. This process has two stages: *goal shifting* and *rule activation*. With goal shifting, the brain is choosing to change its focus from the first task to the second. In rule activation, the brain follows specific rules and procedures that are inherent by nature or learned from experience to perform the task.[25] So first, your brain decides to change jobs, and then it plans and acts to make that happen. These two stages ensure that the brain properly uses its working memory to hold the goals and processes to successfully begin the next task.[26] Your mind goes through this multistep transition anytime you change tasks. This is a lot of effort! This is a tiring process that uses more time than just working on one project to completion.

In 2001, research psychologists Joshua Rubenstein, Kevin Meyer, and Jeffrey Evans conducted a four-part experiment to test the executive control processes of the human mind. The first experiment confirmed that the control and task processes can be separated and affected by different elements. The second experiment shows that executive control consists of two parts: goal shifting and rule activation. The last two experiments show that when people switch between tasks, it can take more time to switch to a task that is less familiar than one that is routine. Therefore, simple routine tasks are easier to jump into than something that you're starting fresh or you're not in the practice of doing on a regular basis. This shows the executive control process in action.[27]

Tasks can be simple or more complex. Examples of simpler tasks are washing the dishes, walking the dog, copying and pasting, data entry, and gathering market research. Some examples of complex tasks are writing a report, preparing an analysis, meeting with a client, or driving a car.

You can see how the executive control process happens in even simple task transitions. For instance, last week I was ordering coffee, and the barista asked for my phone number for my rewards account. At that same moment, I received a notification on my watch for an email. I glanced at it and saw the subject header. This distraction was enough to cause me to pause as I recited my number and try to remember what I was doing.

In a more complex scenario, there are times when I am working on my computer, and my mom calls on the phone, like I described at the beginning of this chapter. She will provide great details about an event she experienced, and I will remember hardly any of it. Looking back, I can tell that, in those moments, I was zoning in and out based on how intensely my work required my focus. My mom has even told me that I tune her out as I'm working.

Society tells me to multitask to get more done. But if multitasking doesn't work, what does work?

Instead of trying to do many complex tasks at once, focus on one task at a time and follow each through to completion. There is no formula to this, which is good. The challenge is forcing yourself to just do it. Don't allow yourself to overthink. Just jump right in.

Finally, eliminate distractions so you can stay focused on the task at hand. What are your holdups? These will be specific to you. Are you too easily distracted by your phone? Are you afraid that someone may need you? Are you constantly being interrupted by family when you try to work in the living room? If your phone is your distraction, then turn it off or move it away from you. If you are afraid that someone may need to reach you, then put up an automatic unavailability notice directing them to someone else. If your family is distracting you, then move into a separate room where your attention can be focused. These are all examples of distractions and solutions. I don't want you to draft a list of distractions. You need to recognize your distractions and find the solutions. If you don't know the solution, experiment with different options until you find what works for you.

My primary distraction is my phone. If I have it near me, I will start to do a million different things instead of work. It's not just emails. I will get on social media for no reason and just scroll. I will get a new business idea and go off on a tangent. Someone will message me a question, and I will take a peek at it, so now I want to address that. Anything. And it's all on my phone. I'm not going to pretend that I've mastered this situation. I still struggle with this today. I cannot work efficiently with my phone near me. I will mute notifications before I start working and put my phone in another room or zipped in a bag.

Productivity is about completing work efficiently, not about doing as many tasks as possible. Take a moment and commit yourself to working on one complex task at a time.

I have learned to not answer the phone while I'm working. Waiting to return calls later, when I can dedicate my attention, is more respectful. I have also learned to set aside time for training and education and not work at that time. Efficiencies are a work in progress and will always need to be refined. There is always room for growth. Keeping an open mind and embracing flexibility will give you the freedom to adapt without stress or anxiety.

## MULTITASKING FOR SIMPLE TASKS

In Chapter 1, we talked about how multitasking can be inefficient, especially for complex tasks. According to Meyer, multitasking can consume up to 40 percent of one's productive time.[28] Still, multitasking for simple tasks can be beneficial and increase productivity, whereas otherwise, it would be thwarted. Multitasking can be used as a management tool and aid efficiencies in certain situations. Simple tasks that require little attention can easily be done at the same time as other activities. For example, watching television while folding laundry can make you feel more productive and isn't going to slow you down. It can also be beneficial in situations where you may not feel as motivated to perform the task, or it may seem kind of boring. Listening to music while exercising can help keep you engaged and give you the motivation to finish the workout, especially if you weren't particularly feeling it that day. Having a phone conversation with a family member while walking the dog is another great example of multitasking. If you aren't working and you aren't pressed for time, the additional time used up multitasking can be worth the benefit of actually making sure the task at hand is done. Sometimes it's more important to get something done than to be the most efficient about it. Especially if you dread it.

## MULTITASKING ON THE PHONE

I work varying hours from day to day. I could be writing an email or doing some light research and studying at a time outside of my regularly scheduled priority work time. My nonpriority tasks and activities, such as administrative tasks, checking and responding to emails, research, training, and even writing, are usually performed at nontraditional hours.

Recently, I was in the middle of writing and on a pretty good roll, and I saw my mom was calling me on the phone. I picked up the phone and had my thumb ready to swipe to answer and almost did twice before I set it back down. I recognized that I was contemplating answering the phone and continuing the work I was doing. I played a few scenarios through my head, trying to determine what research I could start looking up, what notes I could copy over, and what else I could try to do to continue moving forward and answer this phone call simultaneously. I stopped myself and let the phone call go and continue with the progress I was making. I decided to call her back when I got to a stopping point and took the dog for a walk.

I tend to feel like talking on the phone takes away from time that I could be doing something else productive. I am constantly itching to find some way to multitask and be doing something else at the same time as talking on the phone because I feel like it isn't a good enough time filler. The problem with this thinking is that I have tried to add any other kind of task to talking on the phone, and most of the time, it does not work out. Everything else pulls my attention in another direction. Fortunately, walking the dog does not require much attention at all. Calling my mom back and walking the dog have been two activities that work great together. She never complains about me listening when I walk the dog. Keep in mind that this multitasking example is not multitasking actual work. This multitasking is combining other tasks that aren't work related to prevent the urge to multitask during work.

## BURNING COOKIES

One afternoon, I was cooking dinner and cleaning the kitchen and living area. All the food was simmering, I was tidying up here and there, and I decided to bake cookies. I set a timer on the oven when I put them in and began to clean some other rooms, dangerously expanding my reach further away from the kitchen. The timer went off for the cookies, and I looked at the clock and said I'd give it another minute because they usually take a tiny bit of extra time anyway.

I was picking up toys in my daughter's room on the other side of the house and realized that a screw was loose on her dresser. I picked up the knob and fixed the issue, but by that point, I had completely forgotten about the cookies. Five minutes later, I jumped up from the floor in her room and ran to the kitchen because I could smell them. Unfortunately, it was too late for these cookies. They were hard as rocks. I was incredibly disappointed. I recognized that my decisions led me to a place where I had taken on so many small tasks that I lost sight of and completely forgot the original goal of having cookies.

I pushed and stretched myself so far with the number of small tasks I could take on that I started to lose some of them along the way. This is an instance when out of sight, out of mind took over. The cookies were all the way back in the kitchen and completely dropped off my radar. Baking cookies should be an easy activity to multitask. The timer should have been sufficient. However, I tried to do too much at once and allowed myself to get distracted. Cleaning the kitchen and living room, baking cookies, picking up my daughter's toys in her room, and fixing the dresser were altogether too much for me at once. Remember that our minds can only process so much at one time. Multitasking can be a great help for small, mundane tasks, but we still need to consider our bandwidth and how many different things we are processing to multitask successfully. I have learned that I need to actively consider how many different things I am doing at a time and adjust accordingly, even if they are small tasks, because I don't want to burn any more cookies.

## MUNDANE TASKS

Multitasking is great for surviving simple, boring, mundane tasks. For instance, I almost always listen to music when I lift weights and most of the time when I go for a run. I enjoy running, although I often drag myself outside to do it. I really don't enjoy lifting weights, but I know that it's good for me, so I push through anyway. This isn't as miserable as it sounds though. Almost all the time, I feel fantastic after completing both types of workouts. Both workouts are significantly more engaging when I am listening to music. This is especially true for weightlifting because there is almost no chance that I will get it done otherwise.

Multitasking is best used for non-work activities. However, there are some work tasks that can be done while multitasking. Scanning documents is incredibly boring. Periodically, clients will give us paper files that need to be uploaded to our portal. I collect paper files together over time and scan them in bulk periodically to be more efficient. I usually watch television while I scan documents because there's no real active thinking and processing that I need to do, just feeding papers into a machine. If I had to enter data somewhere, then this would not be a good task for multitasking. Scanning documents, though, is mundane and simple and can be easily multitasked.

## MULTITASKING OR WORK AVOIDANCE?

Will cannot stand filling out paperwork. He loves serving his clients through his financial planning business and enjoys the work in and of itself but hates the administrative element. To an extent, manual paperwork can be avoided, but that's not always the case in his line of work. In the past, he listened to the television in the background to better tolerate the work that he was doing as he filled out these forms. However, a lot of very important information goes into these forms, such as Social Security numbers. If he is not fully engaged and enters the wrong information on paperwork to open a financial account, he can have a nasty mess to unwind.

Will discovered paperwork is not a good task for him to multitask. While the task is mundane, it is incredibly important and sensitive. Anytime he completes this paperwork while listening to the news, he must review and check everything multiple times just to make sure that he has entered everything correctly because he knows he is not fully engaged in the task at hand. There is a certain amount of precision required by his occupation as a financial adviser, and it is not OK to enter sensitive information incorrectly.

According to Will, there is a difference between multitasking and avoidance behavior. Avoidance behavior involves a deliberate action to avoid performing a task or other obligation. If he doesn't want to do his paperwork and convinces himself that he can do the paperwork while watching television, then he is maneuvering around his avoidance behavior with the excuse. What he really needs to do is just get the paperwork done right and move on. Before deciding if you should multitask or not, ask yourself if you are considering multitasking because an important task doesn't seem appealing. If the answer is yes, multitasking probably is not going to be the answer for you and could be detrimental to the quality of work you perform. Intention is everything. Multitasking should not be used to avoid tasks.

# Action

Take some time and make a list of tasks that you should multitask and tasks that you should not multitask. Recognizing when multitasking can be beneficial is the first step to implementing productive multitasking into your lifestyle. Here is my list.

To Multitask YES or NO

- Walking the dog—YES
- Reviewing a project—NO
- Writing a book—NO
- Doing laundry—YES
- Sitting in as a guest on a staff-driven meeting—YES
- Explaining a process to a client—NO

# Chapter 7
# Be Flexible

On the 16th anniversary of Hurricane Katrina, Hurricane Ida made landfall in southern Louisiana. The evacuation experience was surreal. Memories of leaving my home at the age of 15, not knowing that I would not be able to return, all rushed back on the 14-hour, bumper-to-bumper drive to Georgia.

Traveling with a six-month-old baby to escape a very possible tragedy was stressful enough. On top of that, I had a business to handle. How would we keep up with projects and serve our clients? At that time, I was the only person working full-time in my firm. Jade was working part-time with me and still in her full-time position elsewhere. My head was spinning.

Society tells us that we need to be constantly active and engaged in some task or activity to be productive. If you aren't doing something with every part of your time, then you aren't doing enough. You haven't put enough into your business, and you aren't competitive. But what about when a hurricane hits? If your schedule is packed, how will you manage? Are you prepared for the unexpected?

There's no set formula for your life or your business because situations change. Change can be both positive and negative. While change can be difficult, it isn't always a bad thing. Change keeps life exciting and challenging. If you live your life thinking that everything needs to follow your plan for you to be successful, then you will struggle significantly when stuff happens. Besides, do you even want to be summed up in a calculation? I don't.

Successful entrepreneurs recognize that flexibility, open-minded thinking, creating space, and planning for contingencies are the best ways to be productive. For example, my colleague Ann sets aside her Fridays for personal care or overflow work and reserves her Thursdays exclusively for contingencies. She has two kids and often requires this extra time to meet her work goals. This has taken a lot of practice. She didn't determine or implement this strategy overnight. You may be thinking, isn't careful planning and dedicating every second of your time to your efficiencies and projects the best thing to do to make sure that you're doing them? The answer is no. It's important to have a schedule and maintain the structure to stay on target, but this also needs to be balanced against the reality that you can't account for everything in life. If you are married to your schedule and hold to it as law, then everything is going to fall apart the second a hurricane hits.

Why is space important? Emergencies occur. You need to plan for contingencies. If you don't have a general plan and the ability to be flexible, your whole plan for order will crumble when emergencies happen. When is the worst time for everything to fall apart? Times of crisis. It's bad when things get messy and disorganized, but it's even worse when your work plan collapses during a disaster situation. Being flexible eases difficult situations.

Everything in life has a balance. There is a time and a place for structure and a time and a place for flexibility and acceptance of change. Structure and flexibility aren't meant to be viewed as black and white nor pitted against each other on a scale. These two elements need to work together in tandem, meaning that you should create and maintain your structured schedule in the corporate space and allow for flexibility in the schedule. You will end up with a product that gives you a sense of comfort and security, knowing what you are doing while also allowing some room.

Don't be afraid of space! You don't need to account for every second of your time. So many people view their lives and their calendars as a color-by-number project, where every single space needs to be assigned a color and filled out to complete the picture. Your life isn't a child's coloring book. This pressure that you feel from society to fill your life is not your fault. This is more noise being pushed at you.

## DO-IT-ALL MENTALITY

Entrepreneurs, myself included, tend to live by a do-it-all mentality. We have so many responsibilities that it can be easy to fall into the trap of handling everything. Maybe I'll feel more accomplished if I do everything . . . It's easier and faster to just do it myself . . . It's just this one time . . . This mindset is toxic to your productivity.

Do you ever reassure yourself that it's OK to schedule a meeting back-to-back because you can be three minutes late, and it won't be a problem? You find some excuse. Then you're 15 minutes late for the next meeting. And so on. Eventually, you aren't anywhere remotely on schedule. Once again, you ask yourself, "Where did the time go?"

Other times, lateness can be inevitable. If you must have meetings back-to-back on occasion, then it is what it is. However, if this is a pattern for you, you are overloading your life and selling yourself short. The do-it-all mentality is leading you to fall behind, so you are later and later.

## CHRONIC TARDINESS

Chronic tardiness is a term generally used to describe this repetitive lateness. According to BioSpace, 1 in 5 people are consistently late to work at least once a week, and approximately 30 percent of Americans are late to work daily.[29] This is a lot of people! If you fall into this category, know that you aren't alone.

Maybe you feel like you just don't have enough time, especially when travel is involved. Or you feel like sometimes your meetings run over a little bit even though you have somewhere else to be. I felt this way. I used to be repetitively late to in-person meetings on the other side of town. It only takes me about 25 minutes to get to where I need to be, so I would just keep that in my head and not really bother my schedule with it. However, this mindset was not working for me. I had one weekly in-person meeting, and although I had the meeting planned, I was consistently five to seven minutes late. I did not account for the 25-minute drive.

Creating time buffers and setting alerts and reminders are key to eliminating travel lateness. Scheduling travel time for meetings is just as important as scheduling the meetings themselves. Now that I block off travel time, I'm not late to meetings as often. I get a notification on my phone or computer when it's time for travel so I can leave when I need to instead of allowing another meeting to run over.

Other causes of chronic lateness are lack of preparation and lack of understanding of the time involved in certain tasks and activities. Being prepared is so important. What clothes am I going to wear tomorrow? What food will I eat? What documents should I bring to this meeting today? What research should I do in advance? You need space to prepare for so many things. I usually prepare for the next day the night before. I gather the information I need available for meetings as well as the items in my daily routine.

Estimations are very important in time management. We need to understand how much time is involved in each task so you can allocate it accordingly and keep your space open. If you find that some tasks are spilling over into other ones, then it may be time to reevaluate how long those tasks take and adjust your schedule accordingly.

These factors are dealt with by every single entrepreneur. You are not alone in this. Refining time management skills takes practice.

# SCHEDULING SPACE

Incorporating space into your schedule is a great way to combat the urge to fill your calendar. Remember in Chapter 3 I shared the importance of taking time for personal care. You need to take care of yourself, or you won't be able to do anything efficiently. You can include space in your schedule by either committing to not scheduling anything at a certain time or by actively scheduling a time block called "Space." I generally block off Fridays on my schedule. I don't actively plan any priority work or schedule any meetings ahead of time for Fridays. Do I work on Fridays? Yes, I do. However, I keep Fridays reserved for carryover work and last-minute or urgent meetings. Here are some examples of items that have fallen on some of my recent Fridays:

- Networking coffee meeting
- Annual A/C maintenance
- New client consult screenshare
- Training webinar
- New software demo screenshare
- Accounting adjustments for a project I ran out of time for on Thursday
- Tax return review I couldn't complete on Wednesday

Some of these tasks and meetings were scheduled because it's an easy day, and they aren't priority work activities. Coffee meetings, training, and research generally should not be done during priority work time, so they were scheduled for Friday. Two of these items were carryover work. The tax return review and the accounting adjustments were both tasks that were designated for other days during the week but couldn't be completed on those days for one reason or another, so they got pushed to Friday. I would never have been able to accomplish all that work if I didn't have space reserved.

---

*Action*

Set aside recurring time for space, whether it's a whole day or four hours. I reserve an hour of work time each working day for contingencies. I don't schedule meetings. I use this exclusively for self-care and overflow work. I understand you may feel like you don't have time for this right now or that you have too much to do. I promise that this will be worth your while. Try setting aside just one chunk of time in a week or a few smaller time blocks during the week and see what a difference it makes in your productivity. Having space for contingencies will reduce your stress.

---

## BE FLEXIBLE

One day, I had a screenshare meeting with my staff accountant regarding some adjustments that needed to be made to a client's financials. I had originally planned to review the financials that morning. After looking through the documentation and having a brief meeting with my team, we found more changes needed to be made before I could review the work. This is OK. This happens. This is why we have a review process. After reviewing everything in our meeting, we planned the adjustments that needed to be made so she could start them. She committed to completing the changes over the next two hours.

When I got off the call, I pulled up my calendar to see how I was going to adjust my schedule. I had a five-mile run scheduled two hours later, after the time I set aside to review this work. I knew that if I waited for her to finish the changes and then reviewed the work, I would have to cancel my run that evening. I decided to swap the two activities in my calendar so everything would still occur, just not in the order originally intended. I immediately got up and went for my run, and by the time I finished all that, the financials were ready for me to review. Being flexible allowed me to accomplish everything I intended in this situation, even though some adjustments were necessary.

Another day, my daughter threw up all over herself and the backseat of the car on the way to school. Sometimes, this is just how it goes with kids. No warning, just sickness. She couldn't go to school. She needed to stay home, cuddled up with her stuffed animal on the couch, resting. I immediately turned the car around and drove back home so I could take care of her. When I pulled up, I got her out of the car first and got her settled inside. Next, I opened my calendar to determine how I was going to handle my schedule for the day. I had priority work planned that needed time reallocation, as well as four meetings to possibly reschedule. I looked at the meetings and decided to postpone three of them to a later date and make one virtual. I looked at the priority work that I intended to do that day and readjusted my schedule, starting with the next day.

Through this planning, I went from having five hours of work for the day to 30 minutes for an easy remote phone call. Taking care of my sick kid was, of course, the priority, but then the second priority was to reallocate my work. Adjusting my schedule and reallocating those tasks as soon as possible helped me eliminate stress and worry about taking care of a sick kid and all the other items on my plate. I was very quickly able to reallocate my work so that I could spend the rest of my time focusing on the emergency in front of me. My flexibility was key to allowing for adjustments.

Initially, when I realized that my daughter was sick, I felt stressed, frustrated, and overwhelmed. I struggled to pull myself out of that mindset so that I could remember what my goal was in all of this. I started a business so that I could work and make a difference in people's lives and still be able to take care of my daughter when she was sick. Yes, it's true that when you are running a business, you don't have sick leave or vacation time delegated to you by some corporate enterprise for these types of situations. This shouldn't mean you don't get that at all. It should mean you have the flexibility to not be limited by what some corporate policy has determined is adequate time for you to take care of yourself and family members as needed.

Do you remember the reason you started your business? Was it to have more flexibility? Was it to be more available for your family? Do you feel more stressed now than before? When confronting an emergency, it's better to take a step back and remind yourself of why you started doing this in the first place. I started my business so that I could work and provide for my family while maintaining a level of independence. As business owners, we can often forget these goals if we don't actively remind ourselves.

## EASY WINS

Flexibility is key to Kim's success as an entrepreneur and legal consultant. She prioritizes her tasks every day to determine what she is going to work on but knows that life happens. She works in order of importance, understanding that not everything will get done. Her goal is to complete 80 percent of the work she sets out to perform. She can still feel accomplished after working all day even if everything doesn't get done in the time and manner she hoped. This is her win each day. What are some ways you can find easy wins in your day? Maybe you can check off one task that you accomplished.

## DISASTER PLANNING

When disasters hit, many business owners scramble to keep everything running. For those who are not prepared, this can seem an impossible task. As I said earlier, when Hurricane Ida hit, my head was spinning. Fortunately, I had systems in place for flexibility and adjusted quickly. First, I checked in with Jade. She was fine. She evacuated to Houston with her family and was eager to do as much work as she could from her current location. Then, I reached out to my clients. I sent a mass email to inform them that we were still actively working on their projects and to provide them with information for disaster relief and assistance. It's difficult to remember much of anything from a time with a newborn in a disaster situation. I prepared at least ten tax returns, among other projects, from my cousin's hunting cabin, using my phone as a hotspot. While I couldn't get as much work done as I would have liked, I did the best that I could as a nomad, trying to stay on top of deadlines without any childcare.

This is an extreme situation. We don't need to live life every day as if a hurricane is coming, but it's still important to prepare for even the most challenging contingencies. Our team had a disaster plan in place. We had the availability and ability to continue working through this difficult situation. With hurricane evacuations, it's difficult to know how long you are going to be out. Sometimes, the storm goes in a different direction or has a lighter impact than expected. Sometimes, like in this case, your power is out for over three weeks, and you must live away from home for a month or longer. Our revenue stream that month wasn't bad. We had our team in place working on recurring and pre-planned projects.

Planning and creating a disaster plan is another way to help you adjust to difficult situations and stay flexible. We had a plan in place for this disaster situation and acted accordingly. Are there any disaster-type situations that could affect your business? How probable are they? Does probability even factor in? If you don't have a disaster plan in place for an emergency that could reasonably happen, you are already set up for failure.

---

*Action*

Take a moment to consider what potential catastrophic events could affect you and your business and write a list. Use this list to determine if there is some kind of disaster plan that you can implement to keep your business running smoothly in the face of extraordinary events.

---

## GIVE YOURSELF GRACE

"If I look at my schedule and it's all meetings, I'm going to get stressed out," Valerie, a successful keynote speaker and business coach, said. "I don't have enough working time to work on the stuff that's due. What I try to do is not overbook myself in meetings because I know that either strategy or working time is going to be cut." Valerie allocates four hours every day to priority work, an hour for strategy or forward-thinking, and two to three hours for meetings. This system helps her ensure that she accomplishes her work goals and avoids stress. "I can flex my schedule that way, but I do have an idea of roughly how much time I need to work on stuff. If I don't, then I'm going to have to work extra hours after work or on weekends. I'm going to start overwhelming myself and start stressing, which is not good." Valerie believes structure is essential to her productivity in her coaching business, but it's also important to stay flexible. "Not every week is going to be a perfect week. I also try to give myself grace."

Do you sometimes feel like you are harder on yourself than on anyone or anything else? Do you feel like you expect more out of yourself and feel like you should be doing all these things? I feel that way sometimes too. A lot of entrepreneurs do. We are so used to everyone telling us that we should be able to do everything and do it all efficiently that we tend to blame ourselves when things go wrong. Valerie is absolutely right. Sometimes, you just need to give yourself some grace. If you are trying your hardest and giving your best effort, the rewards will follow. It takes some time and determination, but in the end, it will be worth it.

# Chapter 8
# When to Hire

"Hi! My name is Jade. I'm an Accountant 1 with the French Market Corporation. I'm in my final semester of grad school at UNO, and I'm thinking about taking the CPA exam when I'm done. I'm excited, anxious, and all the above, honestly, about taking the CPA and furthering my accounting career. Do you have any advice for an up-and-coming accountant?"

Jade reached out to me on Instagram a few years back, seeking advice from CPAs. She was finishing up her master's degree and trying to make decisions regarding the direction in which she wanted to take her career. Her message really stuck with me, and as a professor and young CPA, I really wanted to help her out. I asked her what her goals were.

"Right now, my main goal is to graduate and start studying for the CPA after I'm done," Jade replied. "One of my bigger goals is advising small businesses. I want to be able to move up and get to a point where I can be remote and work from anywhere."

We spoke back and forth for a while, and I offered her a part-time job as a tax preparer. At that time, I wasn't planning for growth or anticipating a need, but this hire opened the opportunity for us to move forward and develop.

When Jade first reached out to me, I wasn't looking to build a team. I wasn't even looking to build a CPA firm. I started taking on clients on the side of my regular work and enjoyed working with people so much that the business just grew from there. I responded to Jade's messages because I admired her passion and pure-heartedness, and I genuinely wanted to help her out. I had no idea that this was the beginning of such an important and meaningful working relationship.

After reviewing my hours worked, I saw I spent over half of my time on tax prep work. I could tell that I really did need a preparer, and Jade filled that role brilliantly. If I had reviewed the numbers sooner, then I would have known sooner and felt less like I was flying blind when making hiring decisions. You may think you're not ready to hire someone or build a team, and that may be true, but in this chapter, I hope you'll look closely at how you spend your time and consider the possibility of hiring someone to help you free up your time—for your well-being, and for growth.

## MY SECOND HIRE

If you are looking to add a staff member, think about what void you are trying to fill. Why are you hiring? Do you have a significant amount of entry-level work that needs to be done? Do you need to offload that work so you can focus on more analytical and higher-level review work? Are you trying to pull out of the daily operations and focus on broader aspects? If these are moves that you are trying to make, then hiring a staff member might be your best move.

Social media is important to my business. I have had clients rave about some of my past content. Many tell me that they looked up my accounts before they booked their consultation with me. I know it's necessary, but I just really don't like doing it. One day, I was scrolling through my phone and realized that I had an entire series of content recorded for social media months ago. These were supposed to be weekly videos. The hard part, creating the content, was already done. The problem was that I wasn't posting it. This was the day that I decided to hire a virtual assistant.

My next move was a Google search. This led me to several different virtual assistant companies, most of which charged a cheap rate because they were overseas. One company asked me what I was looking for in an initial interview, and I really didn't have an answer for them. I told them the story about the videos perpetually waiting to be posted, and they generally understood that I needed social media. However, they still wanted me to spell out exactly what I needed with regard to that portion of the administrative work and everything else. I had no idea what I needed and was really hoping that somebody would tell me, so the meeting ended with some misconceptions that I just wanted a social media manager. I know now that wasn't true.

After that meeting, I noticed I had flagged a message from a colleague's administrative assistant in my inbox a year prior.

This consultation with Christina was very different from the one with the offshore assistants. When we spoke, I told her my story about how I had social media content, and I had no issue creating my own technical information, but I just did not have the time or availability to post consistently. I explained that this wasn't the only administrative task falling through the cracks. I didn't know what I needed, yet I knew that I needed help. She assured me that she could provide all the services that I would need and gave me ideas about things I didn't even know I needed.

I was fortunate enough to find an assistant who was so well-versed in my industry. I also lucked out that she already knew all but one software program that I use. Her services were four times the cost of the offshore assistance but well worth it. I found significant value in the trust she could hold, the experience she carried, her knowledge of my industry, and the programs that I use. I highly recommend finding a virtual assistant who has significant experience in your industry. This has made such a difference in my life. I now have so much more availability and have cut my administrative tasks at least in half. An assistant should be one of the first two hires that you make.

Carefully review candidates for their experience level as well as their skills and qualifications so you can better match your new hire to the level of work involved. If you need a more experienced, technically sound team member, then you need to look for someone with that level of qualification. All candidates need to be screened for general qualities and attributes like problem-solving skills, ability to work well in a team, adaptability, ethics, and integrity, but your staff member needs to meet your business's specific needs to be a successful hire. Fit is everything.

## WHO TO HIRE?

Do you remember my friend Kevin, who also owns a small CPA firm? His first hire was his assistant. His next hire was a part-time staff member. For me, though, my first hire was a part-time staff member. I found that role was more urgent than the administrative role, so I didn't hire an assistant until much later. Your first hire should be either a staff member or an administrative assistant. Your second hire should be for the other position. Both roles take work off your plate so you can focus on completing priority work or growing the business.

What role do I need to fill? How do I determine where my need is? What do I need? Who do I need to hire first or next? How do I know if there even is a need? These are all questions that you may be asking yourself right now. Usually, if you're asking yourself these questions already, then you have been in need for a while. So, how do we determine what your need is? First, consider:

1. What are you doing and how much time are you spending on it?
2. What are you doing that should be done by someone else?
3. What aren't you doing that should be done but fell through the cracks?

Understanding how you currently spend your time and where you may have a need is incredibly important in determining whether you need to hire someone to take on these tasks. How do you know what you are doing and how much time you spend on it? Track your time. So many entrepreneurs, especially those who are solo, don't track their time. I get it. Tracking time is laborious and tiresome. It's my one of my least favorite things to do, second only to billing. It's so necessary, though, and there are many ways to track your time, from using time-keeping software to writing it down.

A lot of entrepreneurs who charge clients hourly for their time already track time. They do a good job of tracking their billable hours but fail to track time spent on other non-billable tasks. I get that too. It's impossible to track every single minute of your time when you do things here and there. Overall, though, you should be able to track most of your time and get a good idea of where it's being spent. Also, your structured schedule should help you cut down on time spent three minutes here and three minutes there until it's every few minutes everywhere. Tracking your time is easier when you aren't constantly working.

You should track your time spent on every client project, whether you bill hourly or not. I understand that it is gravely important to track the time that is billed hourly, but tracking your hours on projects that are value-added or fixed rates is just as important. You need to know how much time you are spending on a project and how much you are making on the project in order to track efficiency. If you are working significantly more hours than you thought you would be when you gave the quote to the client for a fixed-rate project, you are losing money and don't even realize it if you can't track it.

It's also very important to track non-billable, non-client-specific work. Track the time that you spend buying and researching software and training. Track the time you spend on advertising and administrative tasks. This is the easiest way to see where you have a hiring need. For example, if you spend over half of your time on administrative tasks when you have billable work to do, then you have a great need for an administrative assistant. Likewise, if you spend a significant amount of time on entry-level tasks, then you need an entry-level staff member on your team to take on these tasks so you can focus on growing your business. Tracking your time and evaluating it periodically is imperative to know where you are efficient, where you aren't efficient, and where you have a need for another role.

## MY TIME OVER A YEAR ANALYSIS

Over the course of one year, my time was spent as follows:

| | |
|---|---|
| Tax Consulting | 51 percent |
| Accounting | 29 percent |
| Administrative | 20 percent |

At this point, I had a few part-time team members. I still performed 70 percent of the work, and they performed 30 percent of the work. This information showed me that I needed my first full-time hire to be a technical staff member.

*Action*

Add up the hours that you spend on various elements in your business for a period, whether it's a month, quarter, or year. If you have time-tracking software, the data is already there. You can easily pull a report or two that will tell you everything you need to know. Where is your time spent? Does it surprise you? Is your time spent on priority work or busy work? This seems like a lot of work, but you can find out so much about your work allocation needs with these few reports. If you haven't tracked your time already, please start now. Let that be your task. This will give you so much insight into how your work spreads over time.

# WHEN TO HIRE?

If you are wondering if you need help, then you probably already do. Determining when to hire is more of an art. Historically, I have hired after I have been overwhelmed, overworked, and stressed out because I tried to do too much. The best time to hire is after you see a pattern of your schedule getting filled up, but before you are at capacity. This may sound counterproductive, but you should never be at capacity. You may feel like you need to fill your schedule all the time to be efficient, but this actually hurts you. In Chapter 7, we discussed scheduling space and keeping time open for flexibility in emergencies, but that's not the only reason to have space. Hiring when you still have some capacity left allows you the time to train and build up your new team member's skills and confidence to perform their job. This allows you to have room for flexibility for contingencies but also to be able to work with someone new and get them up to speed. If you can sense that your schedule is filling up, it might be a good time to hire someone else.

# ASSIGN TASK ROLES

Review your task list to see what roles these tasks fall under. Are they more administrative? Are they more technical? Are they entry-level? Or advanced? These are all important factors for determining your need. Does this sound familiar? This is just like your structured schedule. Preparing this task analysis on a broader level could be the start of implementing structured schedules for your team. Each of my team members follows the structured work plan, tailored to their own needs. Here are some examples of tasks in my business:

| | |
|---|---|
| • Tax return preparation | • Entry-level technical |
| • Tax return review | • Advanced technical |
| • Tax planning | • Entry-level/advanced technical |

| | |
|---|---|
| • Classifying accounting transactions | • Entry-level/advanced technical |
| • Reconciling bank accounts | • Entry-level technical |
| • Financial statements review | • Advanced technical |
| • Social media management | • Administrative |
| • Billing | • Administrative |
| • Setting up client accounts | • Administrative |
| • Running payroll | • Administrative |
| • Blog posting | • Administrative |

Please note that some tasks may have both entry-level and complex elements.

Once you have identified your tasks and their categories, you can use this to determine what roles need to be filled in your business. This information will help you piece together the job description of your next hire.

---

## Action

What do your business tasks look like? Write a list of tasks and identify what roles they fall under. Don't try to list out all your tasks at once. Just choose 10 to 12 and start with those. Are most of these administrative? Are a lot entry-level? Are these tasks eating up your priority work and technical work time? Is it time to hire? The information you discover could surprise you.

# Chapter 9
# Workload Allocation

"I can do it faster myself." "It will only take a minute to do. Why train someone else? That takes more time." "I can make sure it's done right if I do it." As business owners, we are all plagued by these thoughts. Just because you can get something done faster doesn't mean that you should. You may think that it is more efficient if you do it, but it really isn't. Performing a task faster is not always beneficial. Sometimes, it's better to take more time once so that you can be even more efficient later.

Jade worked with me part-time for two years prior to transitioning to full-time. She and I were both working full-time jobs in addition to working for my business. During this time, I would make corrections to her work and never mention it. This means that she did not know what adjustments needed to be made, and she continued to make the same mistakes. Why did I just make the changes? Because it was faster! This isn't true though. It might have been faster once, but it slowed me down when I had to keep making the same changes hundreds of times.

Once Jade began working full-time, I began to send more projects back to her for revisions—significant changes. After one conversation, I could tell that she was worried about her performance and felt like she let me down. That wasn't the case. I was sending her all the review notes I should have sent her long ago. If anything, I had failed her. Building up your team and improving their skills frees up your time. Allow them to make mistakes and learn from them. This is more efficient than just doing it yourself.

You may be wondering, how do I get out of this do-everything mindset? I get that this can be overwhelming. It's easier if you take it piece by piece. First, understand that you don't have to do it all! In fact, you can't do it all. Nor should you. When you try to handle everything yourself, something will fall through the cracks. We know deep down that we can't do everything. So why are we still trying? What's the holdup? As a business owner, you may feel an obligation to ensure everything is done correctly for peace of mind. The most obvious way to do this is to control everything. That's not easy or feasible. Remember your bandwidth? There's only so much time and energy you have in a day. And that's OK. Believe that your team can do their jobs and stop doing their work in the name of efficiency. Next, allocate.

## YOU ARE THE HEAD OF EVERYTHING

When you start a business, you are the head of every department by default: Marketing, Finance, IT, Operations, HR, Sales, Customer Service, Research, and many more. All you. That's overwhelming! If you applied the corporate structure to your business, you would be the CEO. CEO is Chief Executive Officer, not Chief Everything Officer. Typically, one or more persons are dedicated to these individual roles exclusively. So why should you have to do everything? Well, you shouldn't. And you really can't. You can try, but that isn't efficient.

When I started my business, I did everything. Eventually, I hired Jade. This hire relieved a lot of the prep work and allowed me to focus on business growth. However, there were still tasks that I hoarded. It seemed easier to just do them myself. I let her do the initial prep work for tax returns and data entry work for our ongoing accounting clients. I didn't put in the time and energy needed to train her beyond those basic tasks. I did everything else. I would make all accounting adjustments, analyze the accounting, and review and complete the tax returns. I also handled all accounting cleanup work and special projects. That's a lot. And that's just the technical side of things.

I had no administrative support. I was very conservative and couldn't justify putting up the cost for something I could do myself. I ran all social media, set up meetings, handled client onboarding, printed documents, billed, and held too many other admin jobs to list. I was overwhelmed. I had too much on my plate.

Tasks began to fall through the cracks because there was just too much to do. Social media management was one of these. It's not important to the accounting process. I can get by doing my work without having to use social media. However, an online presence is becoming more and more important to the face of your business.

If you can't be consistent with your posting and involvement, then it's better to not have it at all. If you have an online presence but get busy and stop posting for a while, you reflect a lack of continuity in your business. Current and potential clients could view this as inconsistency or that you aren't really operating your business. While social media really isn't fun or exciting for me, it is still something my clients find valuable. Several times, clients have told me during the onboarding process that they really enjoy my videos on Instagram or the articles that I post online. Pushing this to the wayside seemed harmless but really reflected poorly. While my priority work didn't suffer and clients were well served, I failed to follow through with an important marketing, image-related element of my business. Why? Because I didn't allocate. If I had offloaded some of these tasks, I wouldn't have had an embarrassing gap in my online presence.

## THREE STEPS FOR ALLOCATION

"Eliminate. Automate. Delegate." Remember my colleague, Megan? This is her mantra for workload allocation. This three-step process breaks down the daunting responsibility of determining how work gets done.

1. First, determine whether a certain task needs to get done or not. If not, send it to the trash bin. There is no reason you should waste your time worrying about busywork just for the sake of it. Clearing out anything unnecessary will clean up your task list so you can focus on what really matters.

2. Next, review your tasks and activities for automation potential. Ask yourself: Can this be automated? Can this be recurring? If so, apply your automation tactics from Chapter 5 to those activities.

3. Lastly, allocate the work between you and employees or contractors if you have any.

If you are like me, then staring at a massive list of all the things that need to be done and all the roles that need to be filled is overwhelming. Using a three-step process breaks this overwhelming job down into smaller, more manageable parts until the goal is accomplished. Our goal is to allocate work as effectively and efficiently as possible.

## MY TASK ALLOCATION ANALYSIS

I looked through my to-do list to see what could be allocated. Here are a few examples:

1. I have several continuing education seminars flagged. I have been postponing them for weeks and months. I already have all my continuing education hours for the year, and the holidays are here. I don't need any more, so I eliminated them.

2. I needed to create a newsletter and blog posts. I don't have the capacity to do this ever, so I took a small amount of time to research options. I found that I can create blog and newsletter content through AI programs. I partially automated the content creation through AI and delegated the remaining elements to my new staff accountant and assistant. The staff will do the technical research and create the content, and the assistant will compile and format it.

3. I needed to create onboarding guidelines, but I had been procrastinating. It was easy to put off because I didn't have an external deadline pressuring me. I spent the 45 minutes needed to plan out my content and delegated the production of the onboarding PDF to my assistant.

## Action

Review your task list from Chapter 8. What should be eliminated? What can be automated? What can be delegated? What should be kept? Here is my example:

- Tax return preparation—Delegate
- Tax return review—Keep
- Tax planning—Automate, Delegate, and Keep
- Classifying accounting transactions—Automate and Delegate
- Reconciling bank accounts—Automate and Delegate
- Financial statements review—Delegate and Keep
- Social media management—Automate and Delegate

- Billing—Delegate and Keep
- Setting up client accounts—Delegate
- Running payroll—Delegate and Keep
- Blog posting—Automate and Delegate

Most of the above jobs can be allocated. These are all tasks that I did by myself at one point in time. I did not need to be doing all of those. What tasks are you still doing that should be allocated?

## ALLOCATE THE ADMINISTRATIVE ELEMENT

What value do you provide directly to your clients? "That is what I don't allocate," Valerie told me. "What people are paying me and hiring me to do elevates their leadership skills either through keynoting, coaching, or training. Those are the things people are paying me for." Everything else is fair game for work allocation. Valerie owns a business providing her services as a keynote speaker, executive coach, and trainer. Her key team consists of a virtual assistant, an editor, and an internal book-keeper. She provides the revenue-generating work exclusively.

Valerie *is* her business. Her team takes on the administrative roles so that Valerie can focus on her revenue-generating work:"I want to make my processes more efficient so that I'm working on things that customers are paying me for. If it's something that must get done, then my question is, can I outsource it? That's how I make the distinction of how I can figure out what to offload so I can spend more time and my billable rate working on what customers are paying me for."

Like Valerie, I realized that needed to offload the administrative element of my job. I hired an external virtual assistant and slowly transitioned various responsibilities to her over time. The first to go was social media management. Christina, my assistant, handles all the social media posts. I never worry about it. She sets appointments, onboards clients into our system, bills clients, prints and files tax returns, and much more. I understand that it can be nerve-racking to offload so much valuable and sometimes sensitive confidential work. I felt the same way. I had to start small and then add more responsibilities over time. Easing into transitions may seem unproductive and time-consuming, but if the alternative is to never offload work out of fear, then a slow transition is better than none.

## SHIFTING ROLES AND ADJUSTING FOR EFFICIENCY

No workflow process should ever be stagnant. By this, I mean that allocations can change over time. There are many different reasons to shift roles in your business. If certain team members have been performing well in some areas and want to expand upon that, then different roles may be assigned to them. Likewise, if they aren't as successful in certain roles, they may perform better in a different area.

Another reason to change roles could be the addition of a new team member. I have recently experienced this. Over time, my business has grown from being a small tax prep firm to a more accounting-focused business that also does tax returns. Why has my business shifted so much? When speaking with Jade over time, I have learned that she enjoys the accounting side of her work more than the tax prep. Because of this, I have focused my growth strategies toward building that side of the business. However, by growing that much, there is almost too much accounting work to be done monthly for Jade to handle, plus the tax prep work that still exists. This tells me that it's time to hire someone. Remember from Chapter 8, waiting until there's too much work is too late.

Bringing in a second staff accountant requires workload changes. Our current tax process involves Jade preparing all tax returns and me reviewing them. For our accounting procedures, Jade ensures that all accounting is completed, accounts are reconciled, and adjustments are recorded. I review everything and analyze the financial statements prior to finalization. These arrangements are based on a two-person team. Adding a third person requires adjustments.

At the time of this writing, we are changing our tax prep process to divide the prep work between both staff accountants according to complexity. We are adding a step in our process to determine the complexity of any given tax return. The more experienced preparer will prepare the more complex returns, and the less experienced preparer will prepare the simpler ones. In our accounting process, the new staff accountant will perform the data entry aspect, classify transactions, and reconcile accounts. Then, the more experienced accountant will review everything for accuracy and analyze the financial statements before sending them to me for review. This completely changes the current work process for everyone.

I'm sure that the way I allocate work is not the only way it can be done. There are many possibilities, but this one seemed to fit best with our practice. When bringing in new team members, you will want to look at a few different possibilities for work allocation and possibly test them out before finding the right fit.

## COLLECTIVE ENVIRONMENT

"When I get cohesion and consistency and continuity in this space, I do everything I can to keep talent," Jolie explained. She is the founder of a strategic communications firm, and she has a passion for supporting her team. "I want to retain the folks who are about the work and love the work, so for me, it's about transparency, honesty, and open communication. We all have accountability. I can't be a poor communicator in the space of the profession and expect everybody else to read my mind and do the things that need to be done, so we're in constant communication.

"We are constantly strategizing," Jolie continued. "We're doing brain dumps. We have the think tank, and we spend a lot of time just making sure that we can work smart and not hard. I don't ask anybody in my space to do something I wouldn't do. And secondarily, I'm not a micromanager. We divide and conquer a number of times to get things done. Hybrid-remote work was a culture for us before the pandemic hit. It remains a culture in how we work. It's more efficient." For Jolie's industry, collective work is the norm. Her business culture thrives on togetherness. For her, communication is key to work allocation.

## OUTSOURCING FOR EXPERTISE

In the past, IT consulting firms like Angela's would have everybody you need on staff. Now, you have a core team, but depending on the project, outside businesses would partner with you on the same project, bringing their specialties into the mix. She determines what skill set we are missing per project. Can she partner with another company, or does she have to bring in an individual for this project? In the past, projects were multi-year, but now, projects are more short-term. With more short-term projects becoming the norm, it makes more sense for her to outsource and partner with other businesses on a project-by-project basis.

## RECORDED TRAININGS FOR EFFICIENCY

You may be thinking, I want to hire, but I don't have time to train anyone. Unfortunately, some time will be necessary to dedicate to training new team members, but there are many ways to reduce the time and make it a much more efficient process.

If you don't already have them, workflow procedures should be written and detailed in a convenient location for staff to access them. Most people don't already have this. This is a very time-consuming process, but if you already have at least one team member, delegate it to them. Pick one process each month and have that team member go through it in detail and write out the processes for that task. It may take some time, but eventually, you will have consistent instructions and guidelines for most of your work. These documents can be referred to by anybody going forward and can save a lot of time, especially if updated periodically. Providing a new hire with written processes can be comforting and encouraging and help them get up to speed faster. Even with written procedures, some time will need to be spent walking the new team member through them.

If you have a staff member who can train them or at least explain the processes and explain how they work, you will be able to spend less time on training. Training should not be a responsibility that falls 100 percent on you. If anything, the new team member may benefit more by having their colleague show them the day-to-day operations. Also, when a team member shows a new hire how they work on something in live time, the task may take longer, but the training is accomplished simultaneously. This saves a ton of time!

Finally, training videos are amazing. It could be two minutes, or it could be 20 minutes. You take the time to perform the task once, and then new hires can watch it as often as necessary. You probably just created a training tool that can be used over and over in the future.

I can't even begin to express how beneficial training videos have been in my firm and how much time and energy I have saved by using them. I even make them for clients on various topics now. The best thing is you don't have to explain yourself to different people so many times. If the material is generic enough, you can reuse the same training videos for other clients who have the same questions and save a lot of time.

## HOW DOES MY LIFE LOOK NOW?

I still struggle with the lie that it will be faster if I do it myself. I have to pull myself out of that mentality and focus on the big picture. If I can take extra time to train my team once on a task, then I can focus on something else in the future. If I truly find that the best option is to do it myself, I will make a training video for my team while I perform the task.

As a rule of thumb, I no longer do any prep work. I also no longer adjust projects without sending review notes to my team members. If a change is needed and I make it, I take the time to create review notes. If I don't make the change, I send the task back to the preparer with instructional notes. I create process outlines for everything from tax prep to regular accounting projects and training videos for current and future team members. I also no longer do many admin tasks. Anything I deem important that isn't being done, I assign it out. I spend my time on higher-level review work and specialized admin work only I can do.

## THINK LONG-TERM

Allocation is almost never more efficient or time-saving in the short term. There are significant time savings in the future.

I understand that you may still have some fears about allocation. This is very touchy, especially if sensitive information is involved. Hiring trustworthy, reliable people for your team is key to successful allocation. Forming a strong team that you can delegate work to is the path toward growth and new potential opportunities in your business.

I was sold on Christina before we had our initial meeting. She had experience in the industry and came highly recommended. I casually offered Jade a job through Instagram DMs before she even sent me her résumé because I was so impressed with her drive and motivation. Having the right team in place makes all the difference. Build a team up, and they will deliver.

# Action

Gradually offload tasks from your plate. Choose one to two tasks each week from your Chapter 8 list to allocate and cross them out. Eliminate. Automate. Delegate. I promise you have time to offload one to two tasks right now. Here is another view of my list, showing the since-allocated tasks crossed off. What a game changer!

- ~~Tax return preparation—Delegate~~
- Tax return review—Keep
- Tax planning—Automate, Delegate and Keep
- ~~Classifying accounting transactions—Automate and Delegate~~
- ~~Reconciling bank accounts—Automate and Delegate~~
- Financial statements review—Delegate and Keep
- ~~Social media management—Automate and Delegate~~
- Billing—Delegate and Keep
- ~~Setting up client accounts—Delegate~~
- Running payroll—Delegate and Keep
- Blog posting—Automate and Delegate

# Chapter 10
# Evaluation

In my first year of business, I prepared 24 tax returns. In my second, I prepared 76. That's triple! Triple the revenue—and triple the work.

The first step of my tax prep process is to send out engagement letters. When I started my practice, I used cloud drive folders for everything because they were cheap and easy. Every process was manual. I would create a new engagement letter for each client, copy the standard info, and update the specific client's name, address, and other info. Then, I would send the letter to the client for review and signature via an online signature request function. Altogether, this process took approximately 45 minutes per client. That was before the tax prep had even begun and before the billable time clock started, just to get the contract in place to start the work. This adds up to 18 hours in the first year and 57 in the second year. That's a lot of time to work without getting paid.

How often do you review your major processes for efficiency? Are you living the way I was? Are you pushing forward full throttle, afraid to invest the cost in new systems only to find you have been losing time and money all along? I knew that I could pay for a program that would handle a lot of my manual onboarding tasks, but I put it off because I didn't want to take on the additional cost. A lot of my struggles early on were cost-related and based in my fear to invest in the business.

If you wait until something breaks down before evaluating your business for improvements, you are not alone. I spent two years working through subpar processes before I finally reviewed how everything was going and what the cost was.

Looking into the third year, I knew that something needed to change. If I kept on that path, my business would fall apart. I was working a second job and didn't have time to commit to busywork. I purchased a customer resource management software that incorporated a secure online portal into my business, automating functions I didn't even know were missing. I spent about a week that first year setting up my new systems. Most of this work was a one-time setup that would not recur. In the past, all my work was manual and would need to be completely redone each year. I filed 134 tax returns that third year. If I had continued working under the old system, I would have spent over 100 hours of my time on non-billable engagement letters. Who wants to work 100 hours for free? Not me.

With the new system in place, I spend less than 5 hours each year updating engagement letters that are automatically sent out to the clients. The letters also look more professional.

Throughout year three, I struggled to keep up with billing and chase down clients for invoice payments. My CRM system was off to a good start but not quite sufficient yet. Remember that your systems are only as good as the commands you give them. By this point, I had my automatic engagement letters, but the billing process was still a mess. The first problem was that I did not have a consistent method for billing for all clients. The second problem was my lack of follow-up with clients on invoices. The third problem was the lack of enforcement of payments prior to the services being finalized.

It wasn't uncommon for us to start a project and then either have clients fight and argue over a bill at the end or completely ghost us after receiving a bill for work that had already been performed. This was an internal system issue. I, along with the business, was suffering, and it was my responsibility to correct this. This was obviously a situation that required major changes at the end of the year, but a Band-Aid was still needed to stop the bleeding. I could not wait until the end of the year to resolve this.

I made a commitment to myself to stop doing work without some kind of deposit upfront. This was a struggle with tax returns in progress, so I decided to create progress billings for in-depth tax returns and other projects. This was a bandage. The real solution was the implementation of a formal deposit system for all tax returns and special projects.

The deposit system was officially implemented at the beginning of the fourth year. This solved the billing issue for tax returns and other assignments but not for the ongoing monthly accounting side of our business, which we were actively trying to grow.

Up until this point, we had been sending out invoices every single month, hoping that people would pay in a timely manner. If they didn't, then we'd have to send out emails and call people and get them to pay their invoices. Otherwise, we would stop doing work on their accounts until payments were caught up. This was a very time-consuming and stressful process. I can honestly say that if this were the be-all, end-all, I would not have wanted to continue business ownership. This was a greater struggle than the other billing because this was a recurring ongoing problem. I needed a solution right then.

I implemented a similar automated system for my recurring monthly clients that involved automatic bank withdrawals for their accounting fees. Suddenly, there was no more work chasing people down for payments. I could focus on doing my work. There was nothing I needed to do for the billing period; it was all automated. This was such a game-changer. This was revolutionary. This change was not just another bandage. This was the start of healing.

In our society of always-on, rapidly changing technologies, nothing stays the same. Every system needs constant updates; it can be overwhelming. Realistically, you can't always be changing your systems every second of the day to keep up. That would be counterproductive. At the same time, you also can't ignore that things change over time, and your systems will need to be updated periodically. If you don't have a system in place to ensure that you are regularly evaluating your work processes, you need that now.

Breaking down your evaluation into manageable segments will help you avoid information overload and stress from trying to figure everything out and make changes at the same time. You can break out your analysis in a few different ways. The first breakout is by time. Some processes can be changed more easily and quickly than others. For these shorter processes, you can evaluate them more frequently. For example, if you review your day at the end of each day and prepare for the next day, then you should be able to notice issues like whether you had a difficult time staying focused because you were working in the same room as the television. That is something that you can determine on the same day and adjust so that you can do better the next day.

You can review your entire week at an even higher level and analyze the breakdown of time that you spent on projects. If you find that you spent way too much on tasks that can be delegated, then at the end of the week, you can plan to offload that in the future. You can do even higher-level reviews monthly and then larger system and process reviews on an annual basis. The key is you need to evaluate your business and life for unnecessary or counterproductive elements and eliminate or alleviate them.

## BUSY OR PRODUCTIVE?

Valerie shared her weekly evaluation process. "Was I productive, or was I busy? And there's a big difference because business is an epidemic. Everybody's busy. Period. We're all busy. The question: Is it productive?"

Sometimes, we need to evaluate more than just the tangible elements, like the processes and structures that we use. We also need to review our mindset and make sure that we are on the right path for our vision. If we aren't on the right path, then something needs to change. Does the vision change, or should the path change? If you review your week and see that while you worked a ton, you really didn't get much done, then you may have just been busy. Busy doesn't create value. Busy doesn't pay the bills. Busy doesn't satisfy your clients' needs. If you find that your week was busy but not productive, then you have a clear sign that you need to change something.

## REVIEW YOUR WEEK

Valerie knows what to look out for based on her weekly evaluations. She can get caught up in administrative non-billable work if she's not actively planning otherwise. "On a weekly basis, I look at what I accomplished from a value-added standpoint, based on the effort that I put in. And what's the impact on my organization? What's the impact of my bottom line? My goal is to spend 50 percent of my week on activities that have a high impact. If I did not, it is not a successful week. I have to do something different going forward because, ultimately, I need to be working on stuff where people are paying me."

Filling your work schedule does not equate to success. Having a lot going on is just that. Quality is the most important factor overall. Valerie analyzes her week to see what she did well and where she can improve and incorporates the knowledge she has gained into her next week. This allows her to grow and mature in her business. "Now I also ask: Did I get as much done that I needed to get done? What took the most time? What was the most time-consuming thing that I did? Was I in meetings? Was I blowing something off? Was I choosing not to work by going to lunches, and what am I going to do for the following week to make sure that my productivity increases?"

## REVIEW YOUR DAY

Jessica owns a small CPA firm and a real estate business. At the end of each workday, she reviews her day and plans the next day. She uses this process to evaluate how everything went and what changes she will make going forward. "I have to get at least one productive thing done each day, whether it's writing up a draft report, reviewing clients, or something hard that I can check off."

Jessica's daily review process is not about critiquing her workday, and she certainly doesn't give herself a grade on how well-managed the day was. Her goal is to determine what changes can be made for the better and identify even the smallest of successes. Remember your easy wins. Jessica is looking for her daily successes in this process.

Small check-ins can be great reviews or lead to great reviews as well. You are busy! Sometimes, you may have a really long day and just want to lie down. Should you go through your daily process list? No! You need to recover from your hard work. Instead, take two minutes and ask yourself questions like "How am I doing? What can I do now to best end this day?"

Sometimes, testing out processes will not only show you what works but also where you can go in the future if you take the next step forward. Building on successful tools will make you and your work more productive. For example, our timekeeping software can be very useful, but only if it fits your needs. In my firm, I recently discovered that our current software has some limitations that are affecting our work efficiency. We need to be able to view the total hours per job at any given moment, and the current software does not present this info easily. We are now reviewing other options that have all the functions that we need. By making a change, we will regain the efficiency that we have been lacking thus far.

## PROCESS REVIEW

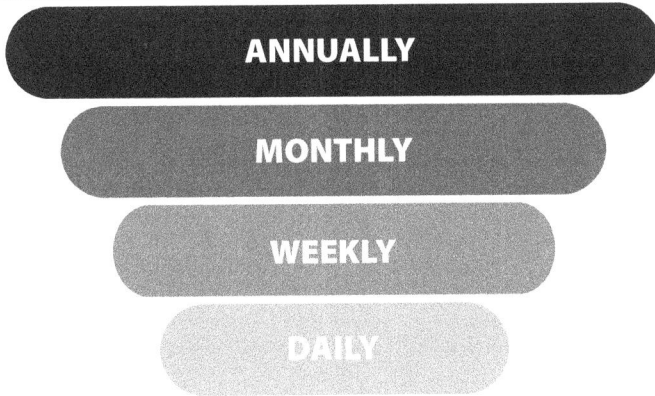

I review my processes in a funnel: broader and less urgent processes are reviewed less regularly than specific, immediate concerns. Let's take a further look at ways to review processes.

**PROCESS REVIEW**

ANNUALLY

MONTHLY

WEEKLY

DAILY

*Action*

Take a moment and identify a few processes to review daily, weekly, monthly, and annually. If you approach the processes with questions, you will have a starting point to solve for the solution.

The more regular processes to review should take less time than the once-in-a-blue-moon ones. Remember to place them in timeframe categories: daily, weekly, monthly/annually. My list follows.

## Daily:

- How quickly and efficiently are you working?
- How well are you prioritizing your work?
- Have you successfully completed at least one task from start to finish?
- Have you taken five minutes to stop and think?

## Weekly:

- Do you have any tasks to delegate?
- Are you performing enough billable work?
- What important work isn't getting done?
- What have you done to take care of yourself this week?

## Monthly/Annually:

- Can any improvements be made to your client onboarding process?
- What potential growth opportunities are available?
- Is there a new product/service you can offer?
- Should you look into a new certification?
- Is it time to consider a new hire?

# ELIMINATE WASTE

Remember our allocation mantra from Chapter 9? Eliminate. Automate. Delegate. This is essentially the same concept. Here, our goal is to eliminate anything that is hindering your success and advancement toward growth opportunities. We want to remove anything counterproductive to your efficiency. The moment that you deem a process unsuccessful, you need to set a calendar event or a reminder to come up with a plan to remove or replace it. Holding on to systems that are failing us is only going to stress you out more and keep you spread too thin. As a business owner, you already have a lot going on. If you know something is not working, rip the Band-Aid off and get rid of it.

Recently, I revamped my onboarding process for new recurring clients. This isn't a process that I adjust often because we are very selective and have a limited number of openings for this type of work. I knew the process wasn't completely efficient, but I didn't bother to change it because of how rarely I onboard a new client in this type of work. Eventually, I had a client call me out about a process that wasn't quite working, and I decided to remove it and adjust the system based on his concern. All our other onboarding processes were streamlined well. The tax preparation process runs itself. This was a straggler. I just hadn't felt the urgency to update the system yet.

Let me tell you how long it took for me to develop a new system for all future recurring client onboarding, including the client I was in the middle of setting up. Twenty minutes. That's all it took. I have no idea why I didn't take the time before to set this up, but it really wasn't complicated at all. Now, I have an easier, more streamlined process going forward to use with my clients.

Each situation is unique, so you will have to determine your elimination timeframe. Depending on the process, you may need to schedule a time in the future that's convenient to remove it, or you may need to cut it out right then and there. Ultimately, you will feel so much relief after removing useless systems from your life.

## WHERE DO I BEGIN?

Reviewing your processes can seem overwhelming, especially if this is the first time you have ever formally done this. You may be wondering, "Where do I even start?" That's a fair question because, unless you break it apart, this can be a very tedious task. Our goal is to make you more efficient without working more, so we want to break this down as simply as possible. If you aren't sure what processes need change or how to change the ones that you know need changing, I have a few tips that can help.

1. Poll your clients.
2. Use your network.
3. Create a trial run.

**Poll your clients.** You may feel like this is an imposition, but I promise this will be worth your while. Your clients will feel valued if you include their opinions in your planning. Gaining your clients' input can help you have an advantage over your competition. You will have better, more valuable market insights and demonstrate that you value your clients' needs and want to solve their problems. You will have improved communication, which will help you foster long-term business relationships based on trust and openness.

In my tax prep process, I send every client a questionnaire that helps guide us to the information we need to prepare the most accurate tax return we can. In the past, this questionnaire was a PDF that was not even a fillable PDF form. While I did not actively poll my clients regarding this questionnaire process, I had one client reach out to me and tell me that the process was tedious for her and that she wanted a different solution. I took her feedback and created a conditional web form questionnaire. She loved it.

While some clients are quick to give you feedback, others won't be as forthright. The best option is to create a poll and send it to your clients. This can be done in many ways. I have polls that are automatically sent after scheduled meetings and after the tax returns are completed. I have gotten a significant amount of feedback through this. Implementing client polls is a great and easy way to gain information on what you are doing well and where you can improve.

**Use your network.** As entrepreneurs, we are the top authority in our businesses. There's no one to answer to. This can be both empowering and intimidating. It's important to have a strong network of like-minded professionals in your industry. I am in a group chat with two close friends, Robin and Seth, who also own CPA firms. We talk daily about everything from accounting or firm-related topics to other personal matters. Anytime one of us has a question or an idea, we bring it to the trio to share with the others and gather our input. Seek out like-minded individuals in your network and see if you can build a trio too. If you don't know where to start, try looking at networking or professional organizations. I met both Robin and Seth through the local CPA society.

**Create a trial run.** Invite your clients and networking contacts to participate in a trial run of a new process you are implementing. A trial run can help you identify weaknesses and correct them prior to implementation. You can refine and improve your system while saving resources and minimizing costs prior to implementation. The feedback you get from trial participants can be invaluable. I certainly would rather critique my process during a test run than suffer embarrassment after the final release.

## WHAT ARE YOUR FEARS?

### FEAR: WORKFLOW DISRUPTION

Will process changes slow or halt the current project workflow? The answer is it depends. It's very possible that you could have to halt certain workflows to make changes. For others, you may not have any disruption at all. If you need to change how you prioritize your work, that will likely not have a significant impact on your workflow and could possibly be completed within an hour. However, if you are migrating to a new client management portal, you need to halt everything in the transition. The good news is that you don't have to make those major changes right away. As long as you set your timeline, you can make these changes over time or ease the transition while still maintaining your current process to make it as seamless as possible. You should plan implementation for major process changes for the best time in your workflow.

## FEAR: TOO BUSY

"I'm already so busy. This seems like so much work to do on top of everything else." It's true that some process changes take longer than others. Sometimes, it's worth it to set aside time to make changes that will give you even more time in the future. Process changes are both short- and long-term focused. Timing is everything. Your evaluation will show you what is more time sensitive. Focus on your daily and weekly evaluations when you are busier. Those are faster. Then, when you are less busy, work on your monthly and annual processes.

## FEAR: TOO EXPENSIVE

There will always be a need for a cost/benefit analysis for major changes. Usually, the more expensive changes are in the larger workflows. For these, you should definitely analyze the costs to see if the changes are worth it. Make sure you include the long-term benefits in your analysis because these larger process changes are usually more costly in the short term but greatly beneficial in the long run.

## FEAR: TEAM RESISTANCE

What if my team hates the new system? I understand this fear. Personally, I have always brought new systems to my team prior to the change to make sure they generally feel comfortable. Some learning curves are unavoidable, but you probably shouldn't invest in a system that your entire team hates. My team spends significantly more time in the operations processes, so their feedback is incredibly important to me.

### FEAR: CLIENT RESISTANCE

What if the clients hate the new system? The question is why. If they hate it because they just don't like change, you may have to work to convince them of the benefits. I wouldn't abandon the system because people are obstinate to change. If there are substantial issues and your clients have concerns, that's a bigger deal. Ultimately, you want to keep your clients happy. Usually, your clients are going to want something that's more efficient, too, because it's more efficient for them. This is a situation where you may need to practice flexibility and understanding.

## ALWAYS A WORK IN PROCESS

My business underwent several large changes in the early stages. This didn't happen all at once though. It was several years of trial and error, failure, then refinement. What did I learn? Well, I realized that my fear of investing in proper systems and improving my workflow processes was hindering my success and delaying my growth potential. For years, I changed bandages and patched flawed systems to just keep going.

After two years as a business owner, I finally evaluated my overall processes and found significant issues. And guess what? It's still not all perfect. Everything is a work in progress. The key to being successful is to have a plan in place to be flexible and adjust. The best way to do this is to regularly evaluate your processes. Rip the bandage off and rebuild stronger.

# Chapter 11
# Don't Procrastinate

"In the speaking business, conferences have hard and fast deadlines for submitting topics. It's automatic, and they just cut it off if you don't meet the deadline." Valerie described her experience submitting a topic for a speaking engagement the evening it was due. She was very comfortable with the topic submission process, so she prioritized other tasks above this deadline. She assumed everything would run smoothly. "It wasn't that I didn't want to do it. It's just I had other stuff that were higher priorities. So I go in there, and it's a new system, and their new system is down. Had I missed that, oh my God, I would have literally jumped out my window. I get so much business out of speaking at this event.

"Why did I wait till the last minute? Why did I do that? I was kicking myself in the teeth for doing that, for waiting until the last minute, having not even looked at the system, and just taking it for granted. 'You've done this a hundred times; you know how to do this.' It's going to be easy, and then getting in there, and it is something completely different. It took three times longer to do it, and it wiped out an entire day for me."

Do you ever feel like this? Many times, it's the simple or routine tasks that get pushed off to later. Have you ever told yourself that you've done this many times before, so it should be easy? You can postpone. I totally get that. It's easy to get caught in a mindset that the simple things can be put off because they won't take very long to do, or they aren't very important. But what happens when something changes and things are more difficult than you expected? Valerie had no idea that the conference she spoke at regularly would change their system before the next deadline. She expected a smooth sailing process and found a completely different situation.

## BURNOUT LEADS TO PROCRASTINATION

I was speaking with Jade about the progression of her CPA exam studies. She told me that while she's usually pretty on target with her schedule, she had a brief period when she was really burnt out and began to procrastinate. Day after day, she would dread this time and put it off to the next day. When she finally got back on track with her schedule, Jade realized that the material wasn't as intimidating as she had feared. She also found that she truly needed a break, and now she was more refreshed. She procrastinated because her mind was telling her that it couldn't handle processing any more new information.

Looking back, she wishes that she had planned a scheduled break. She believes that she may have saved more time by taking a short, scheduled break than by procrastinating over a larger timeframe. The delay caused by her procrastination caused her to consider changing her test date to make up for lost time. At a minimum, she now needs to study for longer each day than previously planned if she does want to keep her original exam date.

When you postpone work, it can feel like a safety net. I do this too. One day, I moved half of everything on my to-do list to "tomorrow," and it felt great—that day. This mindset doesn't help you become successful though. Finding comfort in reasons for not doing your work is counterproductive to your success as an entrepreneur. That fuzzy feeling that accompanies the relief of not having to complete an assignment right now lasts for a little while, and then you face the same issue again, likely wishing that you had just gotten the work done to begin with.

## I DEAL WITH THIS TOO!

I struggle a great deal with procrastination. I was always the student who waited until the last day to study for an exam and to get my homework done. Even now as I am working, I will give myself little reassurances to support myself in not doing what I need to do. How many of these sound familiar to you? Don't worry. You have a few more days to get this done. You didn't get what you needed to be done today finished, but tomorrow is a new day. It'll only take a few hours, so you don't have to start this right away. There's hardly any work right now to do anyway, so don't worry about getting these tasks done because what are you going to do later when you run out of work?

Sure. Things can always get done tomorrow, but tomorrow, there will be another tomorrow and then one after that. Suddenly, you are days down the road with something due tomorrow, and nothing has been done.

What are the tasks I'm putting off? Are they really complicated, difficult, labor-intensive projects? No. Is it something that I don't know how to do? No. The tasks I put off are the easy mundane activities that usually only take a few minutes to get done anyway.

One day, I was reviewing my to-do list for the day and saw that I had a lot of little tasks on it. One task was to adjust payroll amounts for two client employees. I don't know why, but when I saw this task, I immediately dreaded it. As I hovered over that edit task button with my mouse, I paused for a moment and decided to just do it. And guess what? This took 2.5 minutes to finish.

Why was I dreading this? Understanding why we think the way we do is key to solving the problem and finding the cause of our procrastination. I avoid finishing simple tasks because I feel like they aren't a high priority, because they are too simple and can be done later, or because there will be plenty of time later to get them done. At least, that's what I tell myself.

Through a great deal of trial and error, I have come to realize that I have a distorted perception of time. This is one of, if not the largest, of the problems that I have with my procrastination. For instance, if I sat down and planned it out, I would know approximately how long it would take to drive from point A to point B. However, somehow, I always convince myself that I can spend an extra 5 or 10 minutes doing something else and then manage to be on time for another event. It's not logical, and it doesn't work. This is my constant battle. I also always believe there will be more time later. This is a lie though.

Procrastination only leads to a bottleneck of work later. Work is always coming. If you have the availability to get your work done, do it. Don't put it off. You may not have a massive chunk of empty time right now, but at least you won't be overwhelmed, overworked, and panicked in the future.

If you feel like you lean toward procrastination, you are not alone. Procrastination is a big issue for business owners. Fifty percent of all people procrastinate periodically, of which 20–25 percent are identi-fied as chronic procrastinators.[30] That's a lot of people! Putting off work without a valid reason hurts your efficiency. Avoiding procrastination keeps your work from building up.

So, what are some of the reasons that you procrastinate? Could your task seem boring or unpleasant? Do you feel overconfident about the amount of time you have available for work or have a misconception about how much time it takes to get certain tasks done? Does some of your work seem low priority or simple and unattractive? Understand-ing why you procrastinate is the first step to ending the process. Once you know the reason, we can tackle the cause.

*Action*

The four steps below will guide you toward solving your procrastination issues. This is what I call the Procrastination Deterrent Process. Only take a few minutes on each item, as this should not be a time-intensive exercise.

1. Make a list of three to five tasks that you tend to put off.
2. Spend a few minutes on each one and try to determine why you want to put this task off.
3. Try to come up with at least one potential solution that you can implement to avoid procrastination.
4. Test your solution and see if it works. If it does, great! If not, look for a new solution.
5. Create a system to form good habits and foster consistency.

## HERE IS MY LIST

**Reviewing tax returns.** I often dread reviewing tax returns. I feel like it will take a long time and think I can push it off until later when I have priority time available. The problem with this is that an initial review is almost always either returned to the preparer for additional changes or requires more information from the client. Yet I often feel like this initial review will take longer than it does. When I pick up a tax return to review, I usually spend about 5 to 15 minutes on it before sending it elsewhere. To alleviate this misperception, I am dividing out my time for the initial review versus the second review. Understanding the time difference between reviewing the information the client sent and using that information in my work will help keep me from procrastinating that initial review. Reviewing the client's information takes less time than applying that information to their tax return. Sometimes, all that needs to be done in the moment is a quick review to make sure the client actually sent the right documents.

**Creating blog or social media content.** I really struggle with social media. It is time-consuming and strenuous, and oftentimes, people are either pushy with you, trying to sell you stuff, or completely tear you apart. Regarding my accounting firm, social media isn't that big of a deal. Our business is primarily based on our referrals, and we've grown successfully with just that. Although it is important to have a presence online for professional reasons. I mentioned in a previous chapter that my potential leads often come to me raving about my Instagram tax tips videos even though they found me through a referral. They still appreciate the content.

I do believe that creating social media content is important for my business, but it's not important in the same sense that our actual consulting work is. I think that sense of misguided comparisons of priority led me to push it off.

Another reason I avoid my social media tasks is because I have convinced myself somehow that a blog post is an intense ordeal. Realistically, it only takes me 5 to 10 minutes to create a solid blog post for a website. To alleviate these concerns, I created a new time block for media management that I now have on my calendar once a week. I made the commitment to my virtual assistant because she kept asking me for my content, and I kept putting it off.

**Final project billing.** Most of our billing is done via deposits. Every tax return has a deposit one way or another, all our monthly accounts have recurring automated billing, and our special projects have a deposit system as well. Billing has always been a dreaded task for me. Implementing the deposit system and automated recurring payments has helped significantly, but I still dread having to pull reports and determine final billing number figures for our invoices. I combated this by creating a formal task and our pipeline process system for workflow management so this can no longer be pushed off and avoided. I see that if I don't do this, then I am holding up progress for the entire project.

Don't worry if it takes a while to find the right solution for your procrastination issues. There's no one-size-fits-all approach. This is why it's so important to implement these systems and use them to find your unique needs, problems, and solutions. Once you find solutions that work, your next step is to use them. This sounds simple, but I totally understand that it can be more difficult than it seems.

The best way to consistently apply your Procrastination Deterrent Process is to form positive, productive habits. You can walk through the process over and over, but unless you take action and create a habit from repeated behavior, you will fall back into the same procrastinating funk. In my examples above, I detailed my solutions and how those solutions work. What is the key to success in these systems? What do all three solutions have in common? Consistency and accountability. All solutions involve a set practice to accompany the task and a way to maintain responsibility for the completion of these activities. Solidifying a mundane task in the CRM software is a practice of accountability. Making a commitment to my assistant and scheduling time for tasks in my calendar is consistency oriented. Changing my time block naming sequence to change my task misperceptions creates a new positive habit that will lead to success.

## PRACTICE CONSISTENCY

"I'm trying to do more processes. Right now, I have a weekly check-in team virtual call or an in-person meeting on Monday mornings with each team member individually. Most of the time, I was on the phone for 15 minutes, sometimes 30 minutes, if we had an issue. Usually, they would let me know ahead of time, 'Hey, can we focus this week's meeting on this particular client issue that I was seeing last week?'" Jessica explains her weekly check-in process with her team. This practice has not only worked out great for them, but it has also helped her set up her week and plan what both she and her team need to accomplish. When she consistently makes them, these check-in calls have helped her team become more productive and more successful.

Jessica explained further that she was good early in the year at keeping these weekly meetings but, at some point, got off track and didn't keep them up for a while. Her goal now is to get back into having these consistent meetings because they were so beneficial. Maintaining your good habits is just as important as forming them. Jessica created a good system and now needs to consistently follow through in her execution.

What are some practices that you already have in place to maintain consistency? Perhaps you have a regular check-in with your team. Do you have some good ideas for consistent practices that you either haven't yet put in place or you have and just got off track? Maybe you are like Jessica and have a great system and just need to implement and keep it going.

## BALANCING JOBS

Kim divides her time between multiple work activities. She owns a small legal practice and works full-time as a tax practitioner as an employee. Her position is flexible, and she can make her own hours if she gets her 8 hours per day average, achieving 40 hours a week. Kim believes that consistency is key to her success in balancing multiple positions. Although she has flexibility with her hours for her full-time position, she works consistently from 6:00 a.m. to 10:00 a.m. on dedicated work. When she is doing her priority work, she sets her software to show that she is busy so that her colleagues know not to interrupt her.

Do you have other businesses or another job to balance your schedule? What are some ways that you can practice consistency in your schedule working multiple jobs? At some point, you might have had another job before starting your business and had to balance multiple assignments. Or maybe you have been working in your business and have started some other businesses or are looking at new opportunities as well. These are all great reasons to work on consistency and form habits that work for you and your business in tandem.

A system that is not based on consistency will fall apart. I know we previously talked about flexibility and how important it is to be able to adjust to your environment and business needs. This does not combat that at all. Flexibility is important. Finding the balance and knowing where and when to use each is going to be key to your success. Flexibility will help you adapt to unique situations, but consistency will be the backbone of your business success and the glue for all your processes to stick together.

## CUTTING CORNERS VERSUS FINDING SHORTCUTS

As a busy entrepreneur, you want to find the most efficient and effective solution for your work. Accomplishing a goal or finishing an assignment in less time using fewer resources is a dream come true. Naturally, you may want to find the quickest or easiest way to reach your end goal, but the way you get there makes all the difference. There is nothing wrong with saving resources and being more efficient in your work. It's a great tactic for you and your clients.

Often, as business owners, we find ourselves in stressful or time-sensitive situations when decisions, particularly fast decisions, need to be made. In this process, we need to take a step back, no matter how busy we are, and consider our intentions and motivations for the decisions we are about to make. What is the difference between cutting corners and finding shortcuts? This can be a simple, straightforward question when everything is going well. However, when situations become more difficult and more time- or money-sensitive, you may find yourself rushing or desperately trying to find some ways to reach your goal faster.

Overwhelming stress, especially in urgent situations, can cloud your judgment and lead you to make rash decisions with negative consequences. For example, one time I was trying to make some month-end accounting adjustments for a client and wanted to finish faster than usual. Instead of saving the support file in the client folder, I left it in my computer downloads folder. I told myself I would just upload it later. Well, later, it didn't happen, and eventually, I was at year-end trying to find my support document and had to spend even more time hunting through a folder on my computer for this one file.

Cutting corners is a method to complete your work faster that involves foregoing quality, ethics, or other safety factors intentionally. This can lead to significant costs with rework, legal implications, and, ironically enough, more time to complete your work than if you had just done it according to the book. Finding shortcuts involves seeking out more effective and efficient ways to work without making compromises. It utilizes your creativity and innovations that can help you be more successful. Smart choices are made with shortcuts, and reckless choices are made when cutting corners.

## SET YOUR LIMITS

Angelina, owner of an IT firm, was perplexed that none of her proposals were being accepted, especially based on price. "What happened? We kept losing contracts. It's not like we were putting in way over the cost. We were basing it honestly on a 10 percent over the cost, which is low in this industry. Finally, we asked to speak to the contracting officer at one bid about what was going on with our proposal. He said there's no problem with your proposal. It's your price."

She did some research and found that smaller companies were partnering with larger companies to support them and bid low with the intention to either propose changes later or have support to be able to take a loss on the project just to gain a customer down the road. The low bidding for a loss structure did not work for Angelina's business, so she decided to stop pushing resources toward these larger contracts, focus on smaller projects, and partner with larger companies as a sub-contractor. This flexibility has allowed her to recognize and retain the reputation of her business and the services it provides without compromising her integrity or her resources. Angelina stuck with her gut and what she believes without cutting corners or making sacrifices.

Have you ever felt pressure from clients or otherwise to cut corners or allow a practice you otherwise would not have for the sake of getting the work or keeping the client? If you're like me then a large part of your success revolves around client satisfaction. So, what do you do when your client is the one pressuring you to do something unethical? Do you stand your ground? Do you disengage? For me, it all depends. I have had clients suggest some less-than-legal practices, and I very clearly let them know that it was not OK and that I would not do that. I have had some clients get back in line and work within the law, as I insisted. I have had other clients, though, who care more about pushing the limits on what they can or can't do. They don't care about my reputation or my integrity. For those, we part ways.

You may be concerned and have reservations about standing your ground with these matters but there is no client worth losing your soul over. You may be worried that losing a client could be a large loss of revenue. I can tell you that a greater loss of revenue is incurred from legal fees and fines for malpractice or from the strain on your reputation after getting caught up in someone else's messy tactics. You may also have concerns that a client will retaliate against you for standing your ground. While that's always a possibility, I would rather take the risk that someone is going to make a false bad review on the internet than risk damaging my business because I did something I knew was wrong. Regardless, most people who want you to cut corners are not going to harass you or retaliate when you tell them no, and they leave. Why? With their unethical practices, the last thing they want to do is draw attention to themselves. They are in the wrong, and they know it, and if they know better, then they'll just quietly go away.

As hectic as your schedule may be, people thrive on habits. Once you get into the practice of doing something regularly, it's difficult to change that habit. The best choice is to evaluate your habits, make changes, and hold to them. This won't be super easy. This requires dedication and commitment. If you put into practice the techniques that we have discussed, then everything should fall into place for you. Take everything piece by piece, one thing at a time. Your changes will seem much more manageable and less overwhelming. Remember, practice makes perfect.

# Chapter 12
# Fatal Combo

"What are people willing to pay? When we started getting high percentages of yeses, we knew we were too low. We got 90 percent, 100 percent. We started going up on prices until we got to 60 percent."

Will remembers one week early on in his financial planning business when five different individuals signed up for financial plans. Excited for the work and eager to get started with these clients, Will worked diligently to complete their plans. After working 50 hours that week, he looked at his cash clearing for the month and realized that he did not make as much as he should have. At the time, he should have been charging twice as much as he was.

In the financial planning world, the time pressure matters for setup because these financial plans need to be in place as quickly as possible. This created a rush of work all at once. Will was fine with the amount of work but was greatly disappointed with the compensation for the value he had provided. Not only did he undervalue the work to begin with, but he also missed an opportunity to charge a premium for the rush.

Angelina describes her experience with capacity issues. "We had a major deadline to prepare a proposal for more business. Whenever we prepare our proposal, it takes a whole team. Usually, if we have enough time, it's three weeks to prepare it. So, we had that, as well as a few other projects. We were good, though, because we had the three weeks."

In the meantime, one of Angelina's current customers asked for urgent assistance with a project. Angelina wanted to make an impression for continued business, so she agreed to take on the project and start it immediately. "We found out that the customer had another emergency and could not start the job at that time. That was a big problem. This delayed the project another week. Eventually, we reached that last and final week for the submission of the new work proposal, at which point, the current customer called wanting us to start their project."

At this point, the first proposal and the new project needed to be worked on simultaneously. This was not feasible, given their working capacity. "I knew it was my fault because I went in and said, 'Yes, we can do it. Of course, no issue,' which it wasn't. That one-week delay caused such havoc. I know I had to work at least seventy hours."

What is the fatal combo? The *fatal combo* is a phrase I use to describe what occurs when a small business owner overestimates capacity and underestimates value. Like many entrepreneurs, including you and me, Will and Angelina fell into the trap of the fatal combo. They weren't respecting their capacity or their value.

Capacity is how much work you can do. How much time do you have available to work? What is your mental bandwidth? Do you have the means to allocate work? Do you have the resources and tools available to complete the work? All these considerations affect your capacity.

Entrepreneurs, especially those in service-based industries, can easily overestimate capacity. I can say from experience that I often overestimate my capacity because my logical judgment gets clouded by the desire to help people. Why do I do the work I do? To make money and pay for things, sure. But more specifically, why do I do the specific work I do? To help people. I want to help the struggling potential client on the phone, so I want to say yes and take on the engagement even if I really don't have the time to complete the work as efficiently as it should be done.

Value is the worth that you place on your product or services that you are selling. Two major factors that comprise value are your costs and what others are willing to pay. The tough part is that these two elements may not necessarily work together. If the customer is willing to pay and the costs are covered, then great! But if the market price doesn't even cover your current costs, you could be in a pickle. It's better to review this first before you go down a path of perpetual losses.

## SO WHAT'S THE PROBLEM?

If you are overpromising and underdelivering work, you have set higher-than-ordinary expectations for your clients and colleagues, only to produce subpar, disappointing work. If you overextend yourself and aren't even charging appropriately, you will eventually burn out. How do we fix this?

Proper valuation involves accurate pricing and confidence in your stance. Understanding capacity enables smooth, efficient operations and shows you what your current limits are so you can plan accordingly to grow your business.

## HOW DO I DETERMINE VALUE?

1. **Compute your costs.** Simply put, you need to make enough money to cover your operational costs, or your business will go under. This analysis will help you determine what prices you need to charge to avoid losses.

2. **Research the market.** Analyze the competition. What are they charging? Are you on the higher or lower end of market averages? Where do you want to be? What types of clients do you want to serve? Are there any tricks other competitors in your niche are implementing? These are all questions that can be answered with a detailed examination of others in your industry.

3. **Calculate your profit margin.** Covering costs is important, but factoring in room for profit will help you grow a sustainable, profitable business. You need to have the flexibility to handle unknown circumstances. Buffer room will help in the long run.

## HOW DO I DETERMINE CAPACITY?

1. **Evaluate your resources.** What do you currently have to work with? Review the equipment, software, and other tools at your disposal. Look at your labor force. What skills and availability do your team members have? How much time and energy do you and your team have? Remember to review your time and your bandwidth.

2. **Set your boundaries.** Determine how much work you can take on and limit yourself to that level. Your goal is to work as efficiently and effectively as possible without cutting corners or overworking yourself for perfection. We don't want to burn out and make careless errors.

3. **Plan for growth.** Strictly staying within your limitations will certainly keep you from burning out or charging too little, but it doesn't necessarily foster growth. You have to intentionally plan for growth and push your limits bit by bit until you can get more resources to match those capacity requirements.

When I asked Angelina what could have prevented her fatal combo situation, she said, "Well, first, I should have asked the customer if it was really something that needed to be done right now. It's that simple question that could make all the difference. I realize that asking a simple question about the urgency of the task could have made all the difference in how we proceeded. If I had only inquired, we would have been better informed to plan our schedule accordingly.

"The other thing I could have done, honestly, was to ask the team for input: 'I know we have these two deadlines, but we have an opportunity. What do you think about this? How can we do this?' instead of scrambling. I made the decision on my own, and those were the lessons I learned. I promise you I learned them, and, moving forward, it doesn't happen like that." The existing customer project wasn't a priority, nor was it even ready to be done, and it could have been worked on later. Better communication and planning could have led to this conclusion sooner and prevented the havoc that ensued for Angelina.

Will explains his current process and how he has learned and improved. "If you have a rush and I have to put other clients off to work on you, I do factor that into the price," Will says. "I'm better at pricing up front, and when you say I need this done right away, it's not the fact that you rush it that makes the price go up. It's the fact that I don't have time to put this to the side. I have to go and do the hard research right now. I don't have time to wait to ask my expert colleagues in tax, accounting, or legal for advice. I'm going to log additional time to go do the research."

## SELECTIVENESS CAN SOLVE THE FATAL COMBO

"If we're not good at solving your problem, we're going to tell you no. Go someplace else. Many people don't like that stance, and they self-select out, which is perfectly fine. A lot of times, we tell people that we're not going to give them a free financial plan to manage their money like other firms." Will manages capacity through careful selection of his clientele. Like Will, you and I also want to work with the clients we know we can help. If you don't have the expertise in the client's area of need, you should send the client elsewhere. This eliminates capacity issues along with the stressors of trying to do work outside of your comfort zone.

I had a phone call one day with a potential lead seeking tax preparation services. I listened to her explain her needs and the process she hoped for. She wanted to come sit down with the CPA and discuss her documents. She would then leave her documents with the CPA, who would prepare the return and then call her when it was time for her to come back to pick everything up. This is how she worked with her last accountant. She said that she found our business online and saw that we had good reviews, so she was hoping that we could help her.

I explained to her that, while we are a local firm primarily serving clients in our geographical area, we are a 100 percent remote accounting firm and operate virtually. I let her know we meet with clients in person but for connections and networking purposes. All our work is done remotely. I was honest with her, explaining that our method of operations did not seem to meet her needs based on the information she gave me.

After explaining our process to her, she agreed with me, thanked me for talking with her and for being honest and up-front, and said that she would reach out if her circumstances ever changed. Did I land a new client? No. Did I avoid a situation in which I could get trapped doing a significant amount of manual work and lose out on time for other work or for myself? Yes. Being selective and sticking to my boundaries helped prevent me from getting into a situation where I would have likely been overworked, underpaid, and generally very disgruntled.

A major part of selectiveness is the initial client interview. Small business owners, especially in the earlier stages of business growth, often forget that this meeting is not just about the sales pitch to a potential lead. It is an interactive exchange of information for both parties to determine if the business relationship is a good fit or not. Not every interview is going to result in a new business relationship. So many consultants are so focused on landing the client that they forget whether this is a client they even want to partner with. The desire to gain additional work can lead one to make excuses for telltale signs that this will not result in a beneficial business relationship.

Value is the key to a successful business relationship with a client. Does this potential client value your services and the way you provide them? Can you provide the value needed for the client? Answering these questions prior to committing to the business relationship will save you so much time and energy.

If a client values your services, they ask thoughtful questions, showing they trust you and your expertise. They are usually very grateful and openly thankful. If a client does not value your services, they usually start off the conversation asking a lot of questions exclusively about pricing before you can even describe the work you perform. By making a very clear, detailed pitch that sets expectations for the potential client, you clarify all the little questions that they may have. You can then focus on explaining your services and deciding if you feel like the business relationship is a good fit.

The client may not even know exactly what services they need or what they are looking for, so it's important for you, as the expert, to present the client with the services you believe are best for them. Also, you need to be open to the possibility that your services may not be a good fit for the client at all. The relationship may be a bad fit for many reasons. For example, if a client is unable to or refuses to follow your processes and procedures, it's best not to move forward and save a lot of pain and frustration in the future. If a client needs more detailed services than you provide and more time than you are willing to put in, then it likely is not a good fit. There is nothing wrong with walking away from a conversation without closing a deal.

You may be asking, "How does this make me more efficient?" If you close a deal with a client that is a bad fit, you are opening yourself up to a significant amount of trouble down the road. A relationship that is a bad fit will always have tension, and eventually, that tension will lead to either an explosion of events that lead to disengagement or the collapse of your boundaries and procedures. When your boundaries fall, everything you have in place to take your life back from your business begins to fall apart as well.

## MICROMANAGED OUTSOURCED ASSISTANT

Connie provides virtual assistant services using a value pricing system. She charges her clients for the value of the service they are getting, not for any quotas or hourly amounts. If she takes on an engagement to be the virtual front end for a business, she doesn't charge the client for time spent on the phone. Instead, she charges the client for the value of having her team answer any phone call whenever it rings.

Connie has learned that potential leads who ask a significant number of questions and haggle with the price usually turn out to be difficult to work with. She was working with one client who began to call her every hour to check in and then asked for a detailed report on everything done for the entire day at the end of every single workday. The client was trying to micromanage their outsourced virtual assistant. Connie values her services in her expertise in getting administrative tasks completed for clients, taking things off their plate, and making them feel safe and secure that all the administrative tasks are being handled. Eventually, she and this client parted ways, and Connie made changes to her vetting process. She attributes the fiasco with this client to not being selective enough in her potential lead interview process. If she had seen and paid attention to some of the warning signs early on, then she would have realized that she couldn't provide what this client wanted. Vetting your leads is a great way to save heartache in the future and avoid the fatal combo.

## WHAT ARE YOUR FEARS?

Revaluing your business usually involves adding more costs, increasing prices, or both. These are very sensitive tactics in business, and you may have some very valid fears, especially about raising prices.

### FEAR: REVENUE LOSS

You may be afraid that you will lose revenue. Your business could shrink. That's the opposite of what you want. While increasing prices could cause you to lose clients and associated revenue, you are freeing up space for clients who are willing and even glad to pay your prices.

## FEAR: OPPORTUNITY OR GROWTH LOSS

While you may think that you are currently on a solid growth progression, your progress will eventually become stagnant if you aren't charging enough, and you will be overworked. Making room for high-paying clients will create new growth and opportunities, not reduce them.

## FEAR: CUSTOMER PUSHBACK

If your customers push back on your prices, then you may need to explain them. You know your value, especially now, better than anyone else. They may just need to reach the same level of understanding as you. On the other hand, if they are just cheap, do you even want that kind of clientele?

## FEAR: BURNING BRIDGES

Careful wording and attitude are everything. You can raise prices, and a client won't like it, but if you are polite and communicate well, you shouldn't have to burn any bridges with someone who doesn't quite fit your services anymore. I still have former clients who refer me to other potential clients. Unless the situation gets hostile, try your best to part ways on good terms. You never know what opportunities are coming down the pipeline.

## FEAR: UNCERTAINTY

The unknown is always a fear. You can't completely plan for it. There is also uncertainty with keeping your prices as they are. Taking a risk that can put you in a better position is worth it. Focus on your long-term goals. Most of the uncertainty is related to the short term. If you have a good budget, then you should be fine.

## FEAR: NEGATIVE IMAGE

Taking a bold step and standing up for your value should never create a negative public image for you. If a disgruntled client leaves a bad review for you just because you raised prices, that will be quite apparent to the public. Chances are, this will never happen. Most people don't go out of their way to leave malicious reviews. They just go their separate way.

If you ever have gotten into a situation where you were undervalued and overworked, you are not alone. These situations are often riddled with regrets. Angelina regretted taking on too many projects without planning her capacity. Will didn't charge appropriately for his services early on in his business. Connie wished she vetted some clients better in the interview process. What do all three have in common? They have all adjusted their practices and are more efficient now.

I get that valuation and capacity calculation seems intimidating. The good news is that you are not alone, and you don't have to do this yourself. You can even outsource the calculations and the research if you choose to do so. Combating the fatal combo will be the key to your success.

# Conclusion

"Today is not the day for a personal best. Just try to have fun out there."

This was day two of the Goofy Challenge, a Disney World two-day race combination consisting of 13.1 miles one day and 26.2 the next. The temperature was 86 degrees Fahrenheit in January. I didn't care. It was my first time, so anything I did would be my best. As I was not quite awake before dawn, that's all I remember from the Disney pre-race prep talk.

Three. Two. One. Bang! And we were off—20,000 runners and me. I knew what I had committed to do. Still, my legs burned instantly from the day before. Most people never run a marathon. Regardless, I'm pretty sure that no one ever runs their first marathon the day after a half marathon—except me. But that's how life is. You almost never completely recover from the last challenge before the next one falls in your lap.

At 5:30 a.m., we started the race on the highway just outside Epcot in batches. Adrenaline rose inside me as I heard each corral being released into the parks. I had my headphones on, listening to dubstep on my iPod. Yeah, it was 2013. The rush of energy at dawn as I passed through the tolls into Magic Kingdom was like nothing else. I felt the same energy rush when I entered the Disney Speedway racetrack. This was surreal. I'm not a car, but I owned the street. The sun began to rise as the faint outline of the castle in the distance grew closer. How many people experience the sparkling castle at sunrise? How many people are even allowed on the racetrack, much less get to run around it? The price for these one-in-a-lifetime experiences was the pain of running this race. It was definitely worth it.

Running through the parks was amazing, but running between was a different experience. The thrill of traveling through Magic Kingdom, Animal Kingdom, and Epcot lasted as long as we were in each. This race traveled through five major parks but involved a lot of lonely highway time. As soon as we exited each park, I was struck by the reality of the hot and humid Florida air, and almost immediately, the magic was gone. I remembered that I was in the middle of Florida and thought *this is miserable*! The physical exertion and mundane landscape masked my practically immediate memories of the cheering crowds and allure.

In life, we must take the pain with the pleasure. Business is the same way. Nothing will fall into your lap. We take pride in our accomplishments because of the work we put in. Each park was a glorious experience but one I would not have had without the highway time.

Every opportunity and challenge faced is another chance to experience something great or unique, and all these experiences shape who we evolve into over time. This magical experience was a springboard for me to travel for running. Since this marathon, I have run planned races in places like New York, Brussels, and Philadelphia and spontaneous races like a midnight race in Tennessee on a business trip or a race before a total eclipse in the Texas hill country—just because.

What can you do now? You have taken your life back! Maybe you can run a marathon. Maybe you have some other life goals that your business has pushed to the side—until now. You started reading this book seeking more efficiency, but there is so much more. You have learned to care for your mental capacity and set boundaries. You have set consistent schedules that remain flexible. You have created efficiencies by implementing tools and automations and improved your workload allocation. You have learned when to multitask for effective progress. You know when to evaluate and how to avoid the fatal combo.

You now have all the tools you need. The world is yours! What more can you accomplish? You have taken your life back and no longer work 24/7. You have accomplished so much through this journey we have taken together. You are a champion of this race and have built the muscle memory to apply these skills in any new situation.

In business and life, there are opportunities that we can plan for and others that pop up. Building and maintaining the skills needed to succeed in any scenario can make or break your success when the next chance arises, and the only way you can fail is to quit trying.

For a first-timer, 26.2 miles is a lot, especially in the Florida heat! Taking each step one at a time was key to moving forward. I focused on one mile marker at a time for shorter goals. I focused on landmarks I saw in the distance for longer goals. I just needed to get to the next mile marker. I could see the Epcot sphere in the distance. I was aiming for that.

In this book, we have discussed many major changes to apply and many habits that need to be broken. We are changing our entire mindset. Just take it one mile at a time—one magical experience at a time. Cling to the memory of your last success and focus on the next. Remember—there will be a sweaty Florida highway to conquer in between them. But that's OK.

When everything is just a step ahead, the only failure is quitting. My greatest fear when running a race isn't that I'll finish with a poor time or get injured. My fear is that I won't finish. Your race is against yourself. That participation trophy is a first-place prize you win against yourself. That accomplished business goal and that boundary you set to take better care of yourself are prizes you win. Runners pace themselves. Runners fuel themselves. You have your pace and your fuel. You are ready for your marathon!

"Running is magic." The day before my race, I made this shirt in the build-your-own-t-shirt boutique at Downtown Disney. Anything challenging that brings you joy or accomplishment can be magical, too.

What is your marathon? When is your next race? Each consulting project can be a marathon. Each deliverable is a race. Every problem that arises in the process is just another small stretch of a hot, humid highway. Do you have a plan for success? I hope that you take this book as a guide for achieving business freedom and take your time and life back one step at a time.

Your race is against yourself. No one else.

Running is magic. Boundaries are magic. Freedom is magic. Take your life back.

# Notes

1. Sophia Lee, "The History & Evolution of the 40-hour Work Week," *Culture Amp*, https://www.cultureamp.com/blog/40-hour-work-week.

2. "Fair Labor Standards Act Advisor," U.S. Department of Labor, https://webapps.dol.gov/elaws/whd/flsa/screen75.asp.

3. "Defining Work-Life Balance: Energy Is the Missing Ingredient," *Kumanu*, https://www.kumanu.com/defining-work-life-balance-its-history-and-future.

4. Michael Dalton and Jeffrey A. Groen, "Telework during the COVID-19 pandemic: estimates using the 2021 Business Response Survey," *Monthly Labor Review*, U.S. Bureau of Labor Statistics, March 2022, https://doi.org/10.21916/mlr.2022.8.

5. John W. Mitchell, "The State of Hybrid Workplaces in 2024," *Forbes*, January 24, 2024, https://www.forbes.com/sites/forbesbooksauthors/2024/01/24/the-state-of-hybrid-workplaces-in-2024.

6. Jean Moroney, "Dealing with Earned Guilt Loops," *Thinking Directions*, https://www.thinkingdirections.com/dealing-with-earned-guilt-loops

7. Tina D. Bhargava, DrPH., "About Bandwidth," *Everyday Bandwidth*, https://www.everydaybandwidth.com/about-bandwidth.html.

8. Sendhil Mullainathan and Eldar Shafir, "Freeing Up Intelligence," *Scientific American Mind* 25, January/February (2014): 58–63,

https://scholar.harvard.edu/files/sendhil/files/scientificameri-canmind0114-58.pdf.

9. Sendhil Mullainathan and Eldar Shafir, "Freeing Up Intelligence," *Scientific American Mind* 25, January/February (2014): 58–63, https://scholar.harvard.edu/files/sendhil/files/scientific americanmind0114-58.pdf.

10. R. C. Atkinson and R. M. Shiffrin, "Reprint of: Human Memory: A Proposed System and Its Control Processes," *Journal of Memory and Language 136,* (2024): 104479.

11. Mike Oppland, "8 Traits of Flow According to Mihaly Csikszent-mihalyi," *Positive Psychology*, December 16, 2016, https://positive psychology.com/mihaly-csikszentmihalyi-father-of-flow/.

12. Maureen Connolly and Margo Slade, "The United States of Stress," *Everyday Health*, May 7, 2019, https://www.everydayhealth.com/wellness/united-states-of-stress.

13. Ibid.

14. Jennifer Wright, "Social Engagement - A Pathway to Relaxation," *Chelsea Psychology,* https://www.chelseapsychology.com.au/index.php/library/34-social-engagement-could-be-a-pathway-to-relaxation.

15. "Number of Sent and Received E-mails per Day Worldwide from 2017 to 2026," *Statista*, https://www.statista.com/statistics/456500/daily-number-of-e-mails-worldwide.

16. Nikolina Cveticanin, "Wht's On the Other Side of Your Inbox – 20 SPAM Statistics for 2024," *Data Prot*, February 6, 2024, https://dataprot.net/statistics/spam-statistics.

17. "Report: 47 Percent of Internet Traffic Is From Bots," Security Today, May 17, 2023, https://securitytoday.com/articles/2023/05/17/report-47-percent-of-internet-traffic-is-from-bots.aspx.

18. "How Much Time Do Your Employees Spend On Checking Emails?" *PPM Express*, October 19, 2023, https://ppm.express/blog/checking-emails.

19. Alyssa Zacharias, "How context switching hurts your productivity (and how to fix it)," *Notion*, September 27, 2023, https://www.notion.so/blog/context-switching.

20. Gloria Mark, Daniela Gudith, and Urich Klocke. "The cost of interrupted work: more speed and stress," Conference on Human Factors in Computing Systems—Proceedings, (2004): 107-110, https://doi.org/10.1145/1357054.1357072.

21. Gloria Mark, Shamzi Iqbal, Mary Czerwinski, Paul Johns, Sano Akane, and Lutchyn Yuliyas, "Email Duration, Batching and Self-interruption: Patterns of Email Use on Productivity and Stress," In Proceedings of the 2016 CHI Conference on Human Factors in Computing Systems (CHI '16), (2016), https://dl.acm.org/doi/10.1145/2858036.2858262.

22. Henry Cloud and John Townsend, *Boundaries: When to Say Yes, When to Say No to Take Control of Your Life* (Zondervan, 1992).

23. Joshua S. Rubinstein, David E. Meyer, and Jeffrey E. Evans, "Executive Control of Cognitive Processes in Task Switching." *Journal of Experimental Psychology, Human Perception and Performance* 27, no. 4 (2001): 763–797.

24. Ibid.

25. Ibid.

26. Ibid.

27. Ibid.

28. Ibid.

29. "Time Is of the Essence: 9 Ways to Overcome Chronic Lateness at Work," BioSpace, March 15, 2019, https://www.biospace.com/article/time-is-of-the-essence-9-ways-to-overcome-chronic-lateness-at-work.

30. Sam David, "Fascinating Statistics on Procrastination (Based on Research and Surveys)," Proactivity Lab, https://proactivitylab.com/fascinating-statistics-on-procrastination-based-on-research-and-surveys.

# Acknowledgments

*To my family, especially my husband, Chad, and daughter, Miriam:* You always support me and my ever-growing list of ideas and ventures. Thank you for joining me on this thrilling, entrepreneurial roller coaster.

*To AJ Harper and her team at The Top Book Workshop:* You helped me turn my dream into reality through your invaluable expertise. Thank you for taking a chance on me as a first-time author and guiding me on this writing journey.

*To Becky Robinson and her team at Weaving Influence:* Your patience with me being a first-time author and dedication to my book have been key to the success of this launch. I could not have survived the book production process without your commitment.

*To the amazing entrepreneurs who shared their experiences:* I am so grateful to each of you who opened your hearts up to me. Thank you for allowing me to include your life-changing stories in my book.

*To the bold entrepreneurs who read my book in its raw, initial format and participated in the first "No More 24/7" program:* The feedback and support you have given me are priceless.

*To the Top Three Book Workshop author community:* I thank each and every one of you for your immeasurable support, whether it was offering advice on the smallest details like phrasing or providing major encouragement through recommendations and referrals. I am so glad to be a part of this group of wonderful people.

*To you, the reader:* You are the entire reason for this book. Thank you for taking the bold step to take your life back.

*Finally, and most importantly, I thank Jesus Christ, my Lord and Savior, who gave me this vision and dream.* Through You, all things are possible. May this book be used to glorify You.

www.ingramcontent.com/pod-product-compliance
Lightning Source LLC
Chambersburg PA
CBHW071416210326

41597CB00020B/3525